Learning to Live Again

*A practical spiritual guide to coping
with bereavement*

Rita Rogers

PAN BOOKS

First published 2003 by Pan Books
an imprint of Pan Macmillan Ltd
Pan Macmillan, 20 New Wharf Road, London N1 9RR
Basingstoke and Oxford
Associated companies throughout the world
www.panmacmillan.com

ISBN 0 330 41285 X

3 5 7 9 8 6 4 2

A CIP catalogue record for this book is available from
the British Library.

Printed and bound in Great Britain by
Mackays of Chatham plc, Chatham, Kent

For Mandy

Rita Rogers is a medium of Romany origin whose popularity and outreach have exploded not only since her first book was published, the best-selling *Reaching for the Children*, but as her reputation and the respect in which her work is held have grown. Rita can be reached by writing to her at Mill Lane Farm, Mill Lane, Grassmoor, Chesterfield, S42 5AD. She promises to read every letter she receives, but can only reply if a stamped, self-addressed envelope is enclosed.

All the stories included in this book are true. Where permission for stories to be reprinted could not be sought, the names of people have been changed in order to respect privacy.

WHAT IS DEATH?

Death is nothing at all.
I have only slipped away into the next door room.
I am I and you are you.
Whatever we were to each other,
    that we still are.
Call me by my old familiar name.
Speak to me in the easy way
    which you always used.
Put no difference in your tone.
Wear no forced air of solemnity or sorrow.
Laugh as we always laughed
    at the little jokes we enjoyed together.
Play, smile, think of me, pray for me.
Let my name be ever the household word
    that it always was.
Let it be spoken without affect,
    without the trace of a shadow on it.
Life means all that it ever meant.
It is the same that it ever was.
There is absolutely unbroken continuity.
Why should I be out of mind
    because I am out of sight?
        I am waiting for you,
           for an interval,
              somewhere very near,
                just around the corner.
        All is well.

Henry Scott Holland 1847–1918 Canon of St Paul's Cathedral

Contents

Introduction

Having worked as a medium for over forty years I have been able to use my gift to help many thousands of people. Through my contact with the spirit world my readings have reunited many people with loved ones who had passed away. I have been able to use my gift to help people find their soulmates, to help solve mysteries and to save lives. I have assisted both the police and the army with their investigations and have also helped families locate their missing loved ones. But whilst I find all this work both fascinating and rewarding, to me it is nothing compared with the work I am able to do reuniting people with their loved ones who have passed away.

My gift has enabled me to do a great many things throughout my life. We mediums can use our gifts to help people, guide people and look into their futures, but at the end of the day the real reason we have this gift – our vocation, if you like – is to act as a channel of communication between this world and the next.

I have often said that I wished that I had never been given this 'gift'. Being a means of communication between this world and the afterlife can be a strain even at the best of times. I am in effect 'on call' twenty-four hours of the day, seven days a week, which is demanding both emotionally and physically. But when

I read for people who are grief-stricken by the loss of their wife, husband, parent, friend, brother, sister or children and I am able to bring them some kind of peace of mind, then I know that what I do is worthwhile. To be able to tell someone that their loved one is alive and well (albeit in another world), and to be consistently able to prove it by giving specific information and precise details, makes me believe that the insight I have *is* indeed worthy of being called a 'gift'.

Grief is one of the strongest emotions there is and the reason for this is because it is derived from love. Without love there wouldn't be any grief. You do not grieve for those you have not cared for. You do not long for those you haven't loved. It is only when you have loved that you understand what loss really is. And the loss of a loved one cannot only have a profound emotional effect on us, it can actually destroy our lives.

Through my work as a medium I have gained a unique insight into the nature of loss and grief. The majority of people who contact me for readings have done so because they have lost someone very close to them and can't really cope. And if I am honest, the majority of those people who walk through my door or call me probably do so as a last resort because they have found no comfort from the more conventional channels. They might not believe, at first, in what I do. They might not even believe in an afterlife for that matter. But through my readings and by being able to prove that I am indeed in contact with their loved one I can offer them a degree of comfort and a sense of hope.

I am not a psychologist, a qualified therapist or a bereavement counsellor. Am I therefore qualified to help people who have lost a loved one? Well, the answer to that lies primarily with the people I have read for. Each day I receive letters and cards from people all around the world thanking me for their readings. They say how their reading gave them 'hope', 'proof of the existence of an afterlife', and a 'will to live'. I don't claim to be able to 'cure' people of grief, for there is no cure for that kind of pain, nor can I bring loved ones back from the dead, but I can give them the sense that their loved one has not 'died'.

Furthermore, as a daughter, wife, mother, sister, friend and a sixty-year-old woman who has lost a great many loved ones of her own over the years, I feel I have gone through enough of my own personal tragedies to be in a position to help people who are grieving and to understand what they are going through. When you do what I do, it is not enough to just sit there and reel off messages from the spirit world. You have to know how someone might be feeling, as well as listen, care and be there for them.

I have often said that I wish I could read for the whole world. Every day I get hundreds of letters and calls from people all over the world who are suffering deeply from grief and want a reading. Sadly, I can't help them all – it would be physically impossible – and so I have written this book for all the people out there who need help but have no one to turn to. On the face of it, it is a book about grief and bereavement, but it is also a book about coping with that pain and learning to move on and rebuild your life. The message of the book is a positive one and I hope that it will bring comfort and support to many people.

This is an important book for me because helping people who have lost their loved ones really has been – and is – my life's work. With that thought in mind I dedicate it to anyone who has ever been through the terrible pain of losing someone who was close to them.

Rita Rogers, 2002

1. *After Death, After Life*

We fear death because we know so little about it. Dying is a journey into the unknown, one that we make alone, and that terrifies us. But if we knew more about what actually happens when we die, I believe that we wouldn't be so scared of death and dying. If we had proof of the existence of an afterlife, we wouldn't fear death so much. We wouldn't be afraid to die and we wouldn't grieve for our loved ones in such pain when they pass away before us. If we knew more about the 'other side' we wouldn't mourn the loss of a loved one, we would realize that they are happy, at peace and still living, albeit in another world.

Death is the only truth we have. Whatever happens to us in the course of our lives, we know that one day we are going to die. Death is a fact of life. Given that we know this from an early age and have to accept it as inevitable, why do we fear it so much? Why can't we just accept it?

As I have said, much of this fear comes from the fact that we know so little about death and what happens after we die. Much of our anxiety comes from our inability to imagine a world where we no longer exist. It is not so much the dying itself that scares us, but the thought of ceasing to exist. It is the idea that after we die, 'that's it'. It is the fear that there is no life after this. It is the terror of the concept ashes to ashes, dust to dust.

Even people I know who have deep religious beliefs are afraid of death because they still cannot begin to imagine what the afterlife is like and how they will be when they enter that world. Different cultures and religions offer their own interpretations of what happens after we have passed over. Some suggest that the afterlife is divided into a hierarchy of two states of being. Depending on how we have conducted our lives on earth we will either reach heaven or we will be sent to hell. Other religions embrace the concept of reincarnation. Some suggest that there is nothing until the coming of the Saviour. Whatever you believe in and however strong your conviction, it is still natural to be fearful of death because it is a removal from everything we know. Most people, given the choice, would prefer to stay in this world than move on into the unknown.

Death isn't a word I like to use. There is too much finality connected to it. When we think about the word 'death' we think about an ending, a full stop, a line being drawn under something. There is nothing in this word to suggest that there is anything afterwards. But 'death' isn't like this. When we 'die' we don't stop living. Our bodies die but the spirit within us doesn't, it carries on and moves into another dimension. So death to me isn't the end, it's simply a 'passing'. When we pass over, we *pass* from this life into the afterlife.

I grew up believing in an afterlife. I was brought up as a Christian, and was taught that there is life after death. I still believe in those teachings and very much in God. But there is another reason why I believe in the existence of an afterlife that has nothing to do with what I was taught at school, church or by my parents. It has to do with the fact that when I was born I inherited from my Romany grandmother, Mary Alice Thomson, her psychic powers or what some people like to call 'a gift'. My gift gives me the ability to communicate with spirits. When I was growing up the whole idea of having this power terrified me and I fought long and hard to resist it. I didn't want to be a medium, I wanted to be 'normal' and up until I was in my early twenties I did much to avoid confronting this part of my life. I never doubted that people could be gifted in this way – I had seen far too much proof that this was possible from my grandmother, who was a renowned seer – but I didn't want this to be *my* life.

But my head was too full of voices, my mind too full of visions and the premonitions I had were too strong. Eventually I gave in to my calling and accepted that this was to be my destiny. Looking back I am glad that I took this path and learned to use my gift, for not only have I been able to help a great many people over the years but also it has taught me that this isn't just 'it', that there is a life after death. This is proved to me every single time I read for someone. Furthermore, it has taught me that none of us should be afraid of death, but that we should look forward to it, for the life after this one is much better than we could ever imagine.

THE AFTERLIFE

It is difficult to describe the afterlife, for it is not like this world. We are so used to thinking about things in three-dimensional terms that we find it hard to accept that things can exist ethereally or spiritually. The spirit world is not three-dimensional, it is not a 'place', it doesn't have a solid form. It has no geographical location. It is not made up of fluffy white clouds nor is it made from molten rock and flames. It is neither above us, nor below us, it just is.

We cannot measure the spirit world in the way that we measure this world – it is a life and a world without dimensions and limitations. It is super-physical and far superior to anything we know here. The afterlife is like a state of mind. I am not saying that it is just part of our imaginations, but that it is akin to a higher level of consciousness. The spirit world is rather like a dream. When we go to sleep and dream we move away from our physical bodies and into another form of consciousness. In this state of mind we are able to talk to many people and visit them, we travel to other worlds. We still seem to recognize people even though we are not meeting them in person, we have conversations and are capable of emotions. Yet during our dreams nothing affects us physically. We are able to have all sorts of experiences without our bodies. Life in spirit is like this, like another level of consciousness.

How do I know all this, you ask? Well, the world that I am describing is one pieced together from the communications I have had with spirits over the years. I don't claim to have the whole picture; it's only a glimpse, a mixture of fragments of experiences and visions that have been related to me through my readings.

When we die and enter the spirit world we don't go either to heaven or to hell. The spirit world isn't divided up like that with one place for the good and one for the bad. It is divided up into seven astral planes. The first astral plane is for those who have been extremely evil in this life here. It is the lowest plane. The seventh plane, the highest one, is for those who have been spiritually perfect in this life. The planes in between are graded according to how spiritual we are: when we die we are sent to the plane which best reflects how we behaved in this life. The planes are not fixed – we aim in spirit eventually to reach the seventh plane. In order to get there we embark on a journey towards spiritual perfection. Spirits can move between the planes and be with their loved ones in other planes whenever they want. Belonging to a certain plane is like belonging to a class at school – it is not a closed-off place.

Just as spirits are able to travel between the planes they are also able to travel between the spirit world and this world. Spirits come to us during the day because they love and miss us and because they like to watch over us. They don't come all the time, they come when we want them to or when we need them. People are often surprised by this, which is why in readings spirits like to prove to you that they come and see you. They do this by alluding to seemingly trivial domestic details and observations. During a reading it is common for the spirit to refer to something that has happened since their passing to the other side. It could be that they have noticed that you have made a change around the house – you might have moved an object or be redecorating a room. Or they might refer to an event that has just taken place, like a birthday or a wedding, and they will give me small yet significant details of what happened. When I once read for one woman, her husband, who was in spirit, was telling her about the fact that she had a block in her kitchen sink. I could tell she was rather taken aback by this and probably thought to herself, what kind of medium is this! She asked me rather sharply if he didn't have anything more meaningful to say to her, but I tried to explain to her that this *was* meaningful because it proved to her that he came to her and spirits only ever visit out of love. I asked her if it was true about the block, and she went red in the face and said that only that morning she had had to call the plumber out.

When we die our physical body is discarded because it becomes obsolete and isn't needed in the spirit world. In this life we attach a great deal of importance to the human form – we associate who we are with our physical bodies. So when that body dies and ceases to function we assume that our lives are in effect over. But who we are isn't really about our bodies and what is on the outside, it's about what we are within – it's about our souls.

Our soul, our spirit, enters our body at the time of conception and we use this form as our vehicle for life down here. Our soul doesn't die when our body stops living, it carries on. And so when we die we don't *become* spirits; what happens is that our spirit is *set free*. The spirit within us is released and it moves on into the afterlife.

So in death what 'dies' is just our physical shell, our body. The reason why we get so upset about death and are so obsessed with the significance of human form is that throughout our lives we define people by how they look. We talk about people being good-looking, or plain, fat or thin, physically perfect or disabled, black or white and so on. What we look like is supposed to say a lot about who we are. Of course this is true to a certain extent, but it is quite a shallow way of judging someone or getting to know them. This really is taking people at 'face value'.

To know someone really well you have to look beyond that, you have to see them in another way altogether. Only by looking deep into someone's mind and soul will you get to know who they really are, and by doing this you will become blind to how they look. I always say life would be so much easier if we all learned to look at each other in this way. The world would be a much happier and more peaceful place – there would be no racism or prejudice, as a result fewer wars and no one would be seen as 'disabled'.

Our human body is rather like a car. It is a vehicle we use down here. You are its passenger and life here on earth is a road. At birth you are given a brand-new car and as you get older so does the car. Some cars don't last very long because they aren't built that way, and others last for a hundred years. Eventually we come to the end of our road and we can't take the car any further so we get out of the car, leave it where it is and carry on with our journey on foot. That is what happens when we die.

Our spirit and soul are very much alive. When we leave our bodies behind we are still the same people with the same characteristics but we become something else, something far more beautiful and free, like the caterpillar that emerges from its cocoon as a beautiful butterfly. Death is just the chrysalis.

Because we no longer have the appendage of our human form in the afterlife we lose all the problems that our body gave us. We feel no pain, for example, we have no illness, there is no disability and this is why I always say that we are all 'perfect in spirit'. Any imperfections we have suffered down here will be corrected 'in spirit'.

Although they don't have a physical form as such, spirits in the afterlife tend to replicate the appearance they had down here when they show themselves.

But however much you have suffered in this life through illness or disability, in the spirit world you will look just as you should have looked down here had you not been ill. The reason I know this is because when I see a spirit in my mind's eye they always look well and healthy. I also know this because I am able to transfigure spirits. When I do this I summon the spirit I am communicating with and ask them to show themselves to the person I am reading for. If it's to work, the bond between recipient and the spirit must be extremely strong and the spirit must really want to show itself. It is quite a difficult thing to do and it is also very physically draining for me. I close my eyes and blank out my mind; the spirit will then come through. I ask the person I am reading for to stare at me. A hazy mist will start to form around my body and face, and this will take the form of the features of the person in spirit. When I perform a transfiguration, you do not see the actual person who has died; you see their image. If you were to reach out and touch them you wouldn't feel them, and they cannot touch you. It doesn't always work and, as I say, it is quite difficult, but every time I have done this people tell me afterwards that their spirit looked 'perfect'.

But essentially our spirits remain the same as they were down here when they pass over and we will be able to recognize them when we enter the spirit world, the only difference being that they will appear to us looking as they did when they were in their 'prime'. A man who passes over at the age of ninety won't look to his wife who passed over many years before like a withered old man, he will look like he did as she remembered him when they were married. This rule applies to everyone except children. Children who die before the age of twenty-one carry on 'growing' until they reach adulthood. A child who has died at the age of four will carry on growing up until they reach the age of twenty-one. That said, you will still be able to recognize your child when you enter the spirit world. Not only will they come to meet you when you pass over but you will know by their spirit who they are. In spirit we are able to look beyond physical appearance; we are able to look within and to see the soul.

When you die and your spirit leaves your body behind to begin a journey towards the spirit world, it hovers over your body and you begin to travel towards a tunnel. The tunnel itself is dark and you feel like you are being pulled down it towards a pinhole of white light. This light gets bigger and bigger as you move down the tunnel. When you reach the end of the tunnel you emerge in this luminous, almost blinding, white light for a matter of seconds. Then, as this recedes, you see in front of you your loved ones in spirit who have gone before you. As I say, you instantly recognize them. These spirits have come to 'fetch' you and take you into the spirit world. They could be your parents or grandparents, uncles and aunts or your soulmate. If your child predeceased you then they will be there too. If you don't know anyone in spirit you will be fetched by your guardian angel or spirit guide. We each have one of these – they are appointed at our conception – and they will then take us by the hand into the spirit world. Is this just fanciful thinking or really true? Well, the information above is based on my readings and also on my own and many other people's near-death experiences.

Many people who have recorded accounts of near-death experiences talk about having an outer-body experience, being pulled into a black tunnel towards a white light, experiencing a falling sensation and coming out the other side to be met by their loved ones.

One of our greatest fears about death and dying is what it feels like. People who come to me for readings always worry about how their loved one died and whether they were in pain or distress. I can't say that they were not in pain or distress or suffering *before* they died, but I can say that once they have actually died, in other words been declared dead, then they feel nothing at all, just a huge release. And if they have suffered before their death in any way then this will quickly be forgotten. Even when someone has had the most violent death, as soon as their spirit passes from their body then they are free from any hurt, pain or anguish. Again, how do I know this? I know this because at the beginning of any reading spirits will tell me how they passed over and that they are now free from pain and feeling well.

Another thing that bothers many people about death is whether their loved one is cold or lonely in their grave. What you have to remember is that your loved one isn't in the grave – they left for the spirit world at the moment of their death. That coffin, that hole in the ground, that urn of ashes isn't where your loved one is. They are in spirit and all around you. Graves and urns are symbols, nothing more. I always say the grave is for you not for them – you won't find your loved one there, you'll find them by your side, in your house, on your travels, when you need them, so keep looking out for them.

COMMUNICATING WITH SPIRITS

Mediums act as a channel between the spirit world and this world. We are really nothing more than transmitters relaying messages from the other side to people here. The reason why mediums are able to hear these messages is because they have an acute sensitivity.

A medium will either hear a message or will be able to visualize it. If you are able to hear messages you are clairaudient. If you can see them then you are clairvoyant. I am lucky enough to have both of these sensory perceptions, although I tend to use my clairaudient abilities in readings. In order to be able to pick up messages from the spirit world the medium works in close co-operation with their spirit guide. Each medium has a spirit guide and this guide helps them fine-tune their senses and also to locate the spirits that they want to make contact with. My guide is a North American Indian called Running Water and he has been with me since I realized that I had this gift. When I start a reading I will ask him to come forward – I do this in my head, I don't say it out loud – and I ask him to bring the spirits connected to the person I am reading for. Once he has done that and the spirits are with me he leaves me and I start to communicate with the spirits I have before me.

When the medium hears or sees spirits they are using not their physical eyes or ears but their inner sense. The messages that I receive come through my inner ear via my solar plexus, and the sensation is like having a voice in my head which no one else can hear. One reason I can conduct readings over the telephone is because I am clairaudient. When I receive messages from the spirit world the reception can vary quite a lot. Sometimes they come through very strong and clear and at other times they are barely audible. This can be due to a number of factors. A reading might not be very clear because I am distracted by a noise or by something going on in my life – which means that I am not able to focus fully on what I am doing. You can't begin to read for someone if you have something on your mind – it's like trying to have a conversation with someone while worrying about something else. I also have to make sure that I am in good health. People don't realize how physically draining a reading can be: it really does take a lot out of you, so you have to make sure that you are feeling physically, mentally and emotionally strong.

But I find it depends primarily on how close you are to the spirit I am trying to contact. If the bond between you was very strong the messages I get will come through extremely clearly and quickly. If you don't really know the spirit I am contacting then the reading won't be so clear, interesting or significant. I have to admit I am not very keen on reading for people who don't have anyone special in the spirit world. I often get requests from people who want to know about their future – whether they will get rich, whether they should buy a property and so forth. I am not very interested in any of this. I like to use my gift to help people, and if it is my destiny to mediate between this world and the spirit world then I would like to help people who have lost people who they loved very much.

So the readings I do between people who have lost loved ones are always the clearest and the most interesting. This is because the spirit is very keen to make contact with you and communicate something to you. Often these messages are deeply personal, which is why as a rule I never read live on television. When a spirit makes contact with me in a reading it is because they want to talk to you, not a room or studio full of strangers, so they may not come in a situation like this. And even if they do come you have no guarantee what they are going to come out with. It could be quite embarrassing or very, very private, so you might not want other people to hear what the message is.

When I read I do it from the privacy of what I call my reading room. It is a light, peaceful room in my house that has a beautiful view of the Derbyshire valleys and hills. I use this room because it is so quiet, a place where I can relax and concentrate, and a place where spirits want to come. I read for people either in person or over the telephone. Either way the reading is just as strong. Most of the readings I do these days are on the telephone. I read for a lot of people around the world, from America to Australia. This works well, but there are still some people who like to come in person and I find this is good if they are terribly distressed about a death because I can be there to comfort them.

I always like to begin a reading by gently making conversation with the person I am reading for. I do this not to pry into people's lives or to probe them for information. In fact I don't like people to tell me anything about them when I read for them the first time as I find it puts me off. I chat with people because I find it relaxes them. Most people are incredibly nervous the first time they come to visit a medium, which is quite understandable. They can be intimidated by me just because of what I do; they may even be suspicious or sceptical. And even if they do believe in me and what I do, they might be nervous about what is going to happen in the reading. Many people have a lot of preconceptions about what readings are like, ideas they have formed from the television or watching too many late night movies! I don't use a Ouija board, submerge the room into darkness or use my crystal ball. A reading is really just like having a gentle chat, rather like going to see a therapist or even a friend.

At the beginning of the reading I usually chat about something light-hearted like the weather or what I have been up to. I ask only two questions before the reading. The first is what star sign the person I am reading for is. I ask this because I like to be able to gauge what someone's personality is like. This way if I have bad news for them I will know how to break it to them. The second question is whether they know someone in the last five years who has passed over. Now this question is really rhetorical and I ask them not to answer it out loud. I have asked them this so that they will think about that person and by doing so call the spirit itself into the room.

While I am chatting away I will start to get a picture or a voice in my head. Sometimes this might be my spirit guide. At other times, if the bond between the person and the spirit is very strong, spirits will come directly to me. When they do, I will get their voice in my head and it will be as it was down here, so I am able to tell the person whether they had a deep voice or a feminine voice, whether they were foreign or even posh for that matter! They will introduce themselves to me and give me their name. More often than not I will get this quite quickly, but if the reception is bad I may just get an initial to start with and then the name will come to me later on. Sometimes there can be confusion because I am hearing the phonetic sound of the initial, so if the name was Philip, for example, and I only have the initial, then I might say 'F' because what I am hearing is the 'ph' which sounds like 'f'. (Also, I have to confess that I am absolutely rubbish when it comes to spelling!) With the spirit introduced the reading will begin and they will start to tell me things. When I am reading and repeating things back to the person in front of me, sometimes I will talk to them in the first person, at other times these messages will come in the third person. Either way, what I don't do is talk in that spirit's voice or in weird tongues like they do in bad B-movies! And nor do I go into a trance and start shaking. As I say, it's like a very gentle chat, and if at any time the person I am reading for can't cope, then we can stop the reading. A reading doesn't always involve just one spirit; if you have more than one person in spirit they will come too, and they will talk to me and give you messages as well. This can be quite confusing. I once read for this lovely Irish woman and she came from such a large family that she must have had ten brothers and sisters in the spirit world who were all talking to me at once. I couldn't hear a thing. Eventually I had to ask them to all be quiet and talk one at a time!

As I said earlier, readings can be full of the most bizarre and trivial details that aren't all about your future, who you are going to marry and so on. If the spirit knows you are upset about their death they will talk about that. They will tell me how they died and what happened and will do this especially if there has been some question mark over their death. They will also want you to know that they are still with you, that they haven't left you, that they are still alive, and to do this they give you proof. They tend to give me specific details about changes that might have happened around the house since their passing, for example. These details can be quite small. They might have noticed how you have changed the position of a piece of furniture or an ornament, they might tell me how something has gone wrong with the car or that you have recently wallpapered a room. These details often surprise people who come for a reading for the first time. 'That's correct, but why on earth would they want to tell me that?' they say. Well, as I say, they want you to know that they visit you and by giving details about changes in your home or life they can prove this to you. And more importantly they want to give you information that I couldn't possibly have guessed by looking at you. I might, as an intuitive person, be able to tell you that you are happy or depressed, but there is no way I am going to know whether you have redecorated your bathroom – even if you did come to me covered in paint!

But the other thing about spirits is that they love talking about what is going on without them. They will always talk about their funeral, or memorial, or other events that they have been to. This is why I am able to say that I know you have been to a wedding in the last week. I know this because the spirit is telling me so and I can tell you what you were wearing because the spirit was there with you and is describing your outfit to me. They love making personal observations – they will comment on your hair or clothes, tell me that you are expecting a child, or that you are having problems with the children at school. And what's more, they love a good old gossip. If you think about it, a lot has happened since they went away so they like to talk about these things. They will tell you how you are doing at work, what your friends are up to, that you've bought something that was way out of your budget or that you are planning a holiday. People are often amazed by readings and they say to me, 'how on earth did you know that?' Well, I didn't know it. Your spirit knew it and they told me to tell you, and the reason they could do this is because they visit you.

Spirits come and go as they please throughout the day and night. They come to guide you and to make sure you are OK, but most of all they come because they love and miss you.

Julie's story

Because spirits visit us they are aware of how we feel and will know when we are very distressed or upset. Spirits don't like to see us this way and will try to do things to help us. In some cases when the person is very down or in need of help, the spirit will try and get a message to them and they will do this by bringing the person to me. This has happened to me on so many occasions. I find that I end up reading for someone who had no intention of coming to see me – or any other medium. But spirits, as we say, move in mysterious ways and they can be extremely determined. They will try all sorts of things to get you to me no matter what it takes! Recently I was working with my assistant Julie. She had been due a day off but I was very behind with my paperwork so I begged her to do some overtime for me. We were halfway through the day's work and both feeling pretty tired so I decided to make us some coffee to perk ourselves up. I went to the kitchen to make the coffee and while I was in there

I heard a loud cough. I thought it was odd – Julie was down the corridor in the reading room and anyway it was very definitely a man's cough, not a woman's. My partner Mo was out so I knew it couldn't have been him, and other than that the house was empty. I shrugged it off and put the mugs on the tray when it happened again. This time it was as though someone was clearing their throat. Again I ignored it, and carried the tray to the reading room. When I entered the room Julie was sitting there and there was a man standing in the corner. I didn't know this man, I hadn't seen him before. 'About time too!' he said. 'I've been trying to get through to you for days.' He sounded almost irritated! 'My name is Colin, and I died of throat cancer a couple of weeks ago.'

Now, to be honest, I wasn't that taken aback. This type of thing happens to me the whole time but I wasn't so sure how Julie would take the news that we had company! In all the time she had worked for me she had never even had a reading let alone met a spirit. But I knew that this man had come to talk to her. Here she takes up the story in her own words.

I was asked by Rita if I would go into work on my day off to go through some paperwork with her. I had been at work for over an hour when Rita went into the kitchen to make us some coffee. When she came back into the reading room her first words to me were, 'Who is Colin? Do you know anyone called Colin, Julie?'

I said that I did and that in fact I had only been to his funeral a month or so before. I must admit I was rather shocked. I had worked for Rita for almost two years and in all that time no one had 'come through', as she would say, to me.

Colin was a good friend of our family. I had known him for at least twenty-five years, maybe even longer. I was very good friends with both his children – the youngest was one of my bridesmaids at my wedding – and my mother and Colin's wife were also very close.

Rita started telling me that Colin was saying that he had passed away with cancer and that he had left a family behind. She went on to say that his wife was called Pauline and that he wanted her to know that he was all right and free from pain. He said that he had been backwards and forwards from the hospital but now at last he had his dignity back. Rita knew that he didn't like the hospital food and preferred Pauline's dinners, which she cooked every day for him.

Rita mentioned names that I could confirm were correct. She said that one of his daughters had a name beginning with the initial 'L'. I said no to this at first, and then Rita said it wasn't her Christian name but her nickname. Well, Colin's youngest daughter is called Elizabeth, but I had never heard her called that, to us she is always Lizzie. Rita said that his other daughter was called Sarah and that he was mentioning another name beginning with the initial 'J'. Sarah's second name is Jane. He spoke about the dogs that he had, one of them he said he called Oll, and that one of them had been ill. Colin also told Rita that he had met up with his father and that he had found his dog Jip.

During this reading Colin mentioned a lot of things to Rita that I really didn't know about. He talked about odd socks, his maroon pyjamas, 'new windows' and mentioned the names Wilfred and Marjorie, which I didn't recognize. Rita also asked me if Colin had driven a bus but I couldn't remember him doing that. Anyway, I jotted all these things down on an envelope for future reference.

What is strange is that the day before all this happened I had been alone in the house and I had been doing some work for Rita in her office. As I was working I heard a noise – I thought it must be Rita's partner Mo and so I turned my head to see if it was. I had half expected him to be in the passage behind me because the noise had seemed so close, but there was no one there and then I remembered that they were out for the day and that I was on my own. I felt a bit uneasy; the noise had been quite distinct and I hadn't imagined it. I told myself not to be so silly and got on with my work. During the reading Rita said that Colin was apologizing for the fact that he had been there the day before and that he hadn't meant to scare me. Had I known it was Colin I probably wouldn't have been.

I was happy that I heard from Colin but I wasn't sure how to broach the subject with Pauline, his wife. It had only been a short time since Colin had passed away and I wasn't sure how Pauline felt about mediums. It was something we had never spoken about. But I felt in my heart that Colin had gone to so much trouble to pass this message to me that I should tell Pauline about what had happened. I asked my mother for advice and she agreed, so I went to see Pauline.

I was in a bit of a flap when I went to see Pauline. I so wanted to pass on Colin's message to her but I didn't know what reaction I was going to get. Pauline didn't even know that I worked for Rita. But I thought I should try and so I gently told her what had happened and told her about what Colin had said in the reading.

As soon as I said that he had got his dignity back, Pauline nodded and said that she thought he meant he was able to speak again. I asked Pauline about all the things I hadn't understood and had written down. She said that Wilfred was Colin's father and that Marjorie was his mother and that Colin had indeed once driven a bus. The new windows were a reference to the ones that he had planned to put in his garage. And when I mentioned the maroon pyjamas she said that Colin had been wearing them when he died. But it was when I told Pauline about the odd socks that she smiled. She said she had a pile of odd socks that belonged to Colin and that Lizzie had been wearing odd socks when she visited her father in the hospital.

Pauline was a little upset and moved by what I had told her, but she was also glad to have heard from her husband. I think it was a great relief for her to know that Colin was happy and free from pain, that he was with his father and his dog, but most importantly of all that he could talk again.

READING THE SIGNS

You don't have to visit a medium to know that the spirits of your loved ones are all around you. When spirits visit us they like us to know that they are there and so they will often give you signs that they are around. They may do this by moving things around the house, small objects such as ornaments. Or they may start playing around with electrical equipment. Flickering lights, lights which dim or suddenly go brighter or even on and off can all be signs of a spiritual presence.

Many people I have read for have reported instances when their television or radios have been interfered with. Channels change for no reason, radios blast music suddenly even though you haven't turned them on. Kettles suddenly start boiling or your alarm clock goes off in the middle of the night.

People tell me how they feel a blowing sensation on the neck or face or feel that someone is playing with their hair. Others say they can actually smell their spirit from time to time. They will be sitting alone in a room when suddenly they will smell a waft of their spirit's perfume in the air. Others see their spirits in nature in birds that visit them, butterflies and cats, in flowers, which suddenly bloom out of season.

But perhaps the most common time we sense a spirit is when we are dreaming. Spirits do like to visit us at night, just to watch over us while we sleep. When this happens we tend to be aware of this and so we dream of the person who has passed over. Often these dreams are so vivid that when we wake we feel so close to them and so strongly that we have been with them that we have to remind ourselves that they are dead and we were dreaming.

If you have loved someone who has passed over, look out for these signs and, most importantly of all, remember this – that even though you cannot hear or see your spirit, that does not mean that they are not with you.

2. *The Grieving Process*

We might think we know what grief is. We may have watched other people we know go through it. We may feel that we understand what this emotion is all about, but the fact is that unless you have gone through it you cannot possibly begin to understand this very complex and traumatic of emotions. When we think of people being grief-stricken we tend to think of them as being intensely sad or depressed. But grief is much more complicated than that. It isn't just one emotion. It isn't just about sadness. 'Grief' is an umbrella term for a whole range of emotions such as numbness, shock, denial, depression, anxiety, guilt, emptiness, numbness and, finally, acceptance. And when we grieve we don't just experience one of these emotions. Over time, as the pain sinks in, we may experience many of these emotions – sometimes all of them at once.

There is no blueprint for grief, it doesn't follow any particular pattern. These emotions do not follow any sequence, they come and go at different times. When we lose a loved one we ride an emotional roller coaster into the unknown. The fact is, however much we prepare for the death of someone, we can never prepare ourselves for the aftershock of emotions that follows the loss of someone we love.

None of us grieves in the same way. How we grieve and what

we feel when we lose a loved one will depend on a number of factors. It may depend on how someone died, for example. If a thirty-year-old man is killed in a car accident, people close to him may go into shock first of all, because up until the day he died he was a fit and healthy man, and no one was prepared for his death. His parents might feel angry towards the driver of the other car and need someone to blame. His contemporaries might become depressed because his death has made them aware of their own mortality. His girlfriend might feel guilty because it was she who asked him to drive to the shops that evening, and so on.

If a fifty-year-old woman loses her long battle with cancer, her husband who has been caring for her might feel relieved. Not relieved that she is dead, relieved that she is no longer suffering. But their children may feel angry about the death because they have been deprived of their mother. Her sister might feel numbed by her death because, having spent so much time with her before she died, there is now a hole in her life.

How we react to death depends on the way in which our loved one died and, more importantly, on our relationship with that person. Let's take a situation from one of my case histories.

A family lose a young teenage child in a car crash. The mother has gone into shock and as a result is unable to communicate her emotions to the rest of her family. She sits in silence and is unable to move or express herself in any way to the people around her. The father, on the other hand, will talk of little else. His emotions are running high, he is very vocal and is becoming angry. He goes through the events leading to his son's death again and again. The angrier he gets the more he needs someone to blame. The eldest son seems on the face of it very calm and in control. For the next few days and weeks he makes arrangements for the funeral, the flowers, the announcement, he deals with the callers and well-wishers and the order of service. The middle child, the daughter, busies herself with domestic chores. She cooks, cleans, sometimes to the point of obsession, and keeps the home front going. The mother's sister is tearful, the father's sister talks about clearing the boy's room, whilst the grandfather seems racked with guilt, believing that somehow it is his fault, that he should have been the next 'to go'.

The situation I have just described is based on a true story from a reading I did recently, but it is, in fact, quite typical of what happens when a family lose a loved one. All these people are united by the sudden unexpected loss of the boy, and each in their own way is suffering immensely. Yet each of them is doing it in different ways, because within any family people tend to adopt different roles.

The mother is understandably shocked. She has lost her baby boy. The natural order of life has been broken and such is her distress that she is unable to articulate the emotions she is going through. The father takes on the responsible male role. He counterbalances his wife's internalized state of mind by being pragmatic and vocal. He adopts the stance of head of the family by actively looking for answers, blame and retribution. He copes with the news of his son's death by trying to 'put things right'. As the parents go through these states the elder children take on what they see as their parents' traditional roles. The elder son becomes the 'fixer'. By becoming practical he feels he is engaged in what is going on, but in fact is distracting himself. Likewise the daughter eases the family's and her own pain by busying herself with the running of the house. She is on autopilot. It is a cry for the restoration of order, an unconscious longing for things to go back to how they were before the accident; in other words, she is wishing her brother would return.

The mother's sister is tearful not just for the loss of her nephew but most probably also for her sister. The father's sister is going through a denial stage. By suggesting that at some stage the boy's room should be cleared, far from being callous, she is trying to make their pain go away. The grandfather feels guilty, even though there was nothing he could have done to prevent the accident, because he realizes that, as an old man, it should have been him who died, given that he has already lived his life, not a thirteen-year-old boy.

As time goes on these roles will shift and the family will go through different stages of grief. The aunts will adopt more practical roles. The grandfather might become deeply saddened and introverted. The daughter will become more emotional, anxious even. The brother, left with nothing practical to do after the funeral, will go through a stage of emptiness before feeling the ultimate pain of his younger brother's death. The father, exhausted by the energy he projected as anger, will become introverted whilst the mother will begin to become more expressive in her sadness and loss. As the others move back into their lives she realizes that it will not be so easy for her and that she will be in mourning for the rest of her life. She wants to talk about her son, wants to have portraits painted, but her husband doesn't want to talk about it. He is hurting but cannot express the pain. The couple are in danger of drifting apart and they should be aware of this: as I say to people when they lose a child, don't bury your wedding rings along with your child.

When I read for people who are grieving I always try to make them well aware of what lies ahead and also to remind them that we all grieve in different ways. There is a danger in family situations of not being aware of how other people might be feeling. Just because they aren't crying doesn't mean that they don't care. Just because they have gone back to work or are trying to lead a normal social life doesn't mean that the death hasn't affected them. It has. It's just that this is their way of dealing with it. We must never judge other people at times like this. Each of us has a different way of coping with loss and tragedy.

This is particularly true when it comes to men and women. Men and women react to life in completely different ways as it is, so when it comes to losing a loved one don't expect that to change. I always try to drill this into couples I read for, especially when they have lost a child. In my experience as both a medium and as a woman, women are much more 'emotional' than men. I am not saying that they feel the death or loss any more than a man would, but they show their emotions more readily. Men tend to be more stoic and more practical. Within a marriage this is a role the husband will adopt quickly in an unconscious attempt to help the wife, but often this strength is just a show, and deep down they are breaking up inside. Women are much more used to showing emotions and also, significantly, better at understanding them. I read for many more women than I do men, because women aren't afraid to come to someone like me. They don't mind what people think, they will do anything they can to make themselves feel better. Men are much more reluctant. They might feel that it isn't the 'right thing to do'. They usually think that people just have to 'get on with things'. The funny thing about this is that when men are dragged reluctantly into my reading room by their wives, they are always the ones who are much more tearful and emotional!

I try to warn women in situations like these not to think that they have the monopoly on grief or pain. It is very important to understand that your husband is suffering too and, for that matter, all of your family. It is crucial not to alienate anyone around you at this time, not only because you need them but also because they need you. We have to be strong for each other. If death teaches us anything at all then it's how much we love each other. So when you lose a loved one, keep reminding yourself of this and appreciate what you still have. This is very important if you lose a child but have other children still living. Obviously the pain we suffer when we lose a child is intense, but it is crucial not to forget that you have other children. You must be aware that they are grieving too and that they need your love. Time and time again I have seen the child that is left feeling isolated and unloved. They can end up believing that you would rather they were dead, and this can lead to a jealousy of the child that has passed away.

THE GRIEVING PROCESS

In this section I want to take you through the various emotions that you can expect to go through when you lose someone you love. As I have said, the grieving process does not follow a sequential pattern so I have listed them alphabetically.

Anger

Whether you lose someone you love in a sudden accident or through long illness, it is very common for you at some stage to feel anger. This anger could be directed at the person you think is responsible for the death, or at someone close to you, as I'm afraid that when we are upset we tend to take it out on the people we love most. It is very normal to want to blame someone when you are hurt. Anger is an outlet and it can be quite a cathartic way of channelling your hurt, distress and confusion. But what I want you to remember is that, unless someone is directly responsible for the death of your loved one, what you are really angry about is that the person you love is no longer with you. So before you hit out at someone, take a deep breath and think of this.

Anxiety

The stress of losing someone close to you can make you feel incredibly anxious. You may feel lost and wonder how you are going to cope without them. I find that people who lose soul-mates are especially prone to this. A husband or wife may worry about how they will survive without the other purely on a domestic level, and the reason for this is because they have spent so much time together. If we have relied heavily on someone in our lives their death can have a terribly disabling effect on us. We may suffer from anxiety attacks, may wake up late at night wondering how we are going to cope and may be completely unable to function because of our loss. We have to learn that whilst we now have to become independent there are others around us who will help us, and we have to learn to ask for that support and help.

Denial

A lot of people go into denial when they lose a loved one. This may start quite simply when the morning after you have heard the news you wake up and think that you must have been dreaming, or in an unconscious state you forget what has happened. When people have been very much part of our lives it is very difficult to get used to the fact that they are no longer with us. We have to change our routines and that can be hard to do when we are already very upset, so we end up laying the table for them, buying them presents, ringing them up. People who go through this aren't going mad, they are simply taking their time to adjust to the death. Of course, there are situations when denial becomes more extreme and people really will not accept that their loved one is dead. In cases like this it is very important to treat them with kid gloves because they have gone into a mental state of shock. You need to introduce the subject of the death gently but often, until they finally accept it as a reality. If this doesn't work you should consult their doctor.

Depression

It is very normal for people to suffer depression for years after a death. I find that we don't get depressed early on in the grieving process because we are going through too many other emotions, but once we have been through these we do tend to become withdrawn and depressed. There are many symptoms of depression, which include an inability to get out of bed, a loss of interest in most things to do with your life, a loss of sex drive and low self-esteem. Depression is an illness and is something that can be cased with the right medication or the help of a therapist. It is not something that we should have to deal with on our own, and if you are suffering from depression you really should consult a doctor.

Drink

People turn to the bottle when they lose someone close to them in order to escape reality. I have known mothers who normally barely get through a glass of white wine at a party hit the bottle very hard when they lose a child. I can see why people do this, or even resort to drugs, because it causes a suspension of reality and it numbs the pain. The problem is, though, that it does far more harm than good. While you might feel fine drowning your sorrows, think what you will feel like when the effects of the alcohol wear off. The fact is, however awful it seems, at some stage you are going to have to accept the death and face reality. Drinking really isn't the answer and, furthermore, it can destroy what you have left of your life and your other relationships.

Emptiness

Feeling empty after someone dies is very common. Usually this happens after we have gone through the initial drama of the death and the funeral. Once that is over we may feel that we have nothing left. The loss of our loved one has created a void in our lives and we are now left with a huge amount of time, and nothing to fill it with. Feelings of emptiness particularly affect those who have nursed people through illness. So much of their time has been taken up with it that they are left with a huge gap in their lives.

Once the person you loved has been buried, you will come face to face with your situation and this will leave you feeling very lonely and empty. To address this problem try and do something very positive to get you through this stage. You could try and do something for yourself or for the memory of the one that has gone. Either way, it is good to find a project that will help you put one foot in front of the other.

Guilt

I think this is the most common emotion we go through when we lose a loved one. No matter how irrational it may be, we always think that somehow we could have done something to prevent their death. This is particularly prevalent in cases of suicide, when a child dies or with an accidental death.

Guilt is a very normal human reaction to go through, but sometimes we punish ourselves too much. We have to remember that death is really out of our hands. It is something that has been destined to happen and there really isn't that much we can do to prevent it if that person's time has come. If I had a penny for every time someone has said to me they could have prevented it, or seen the signs, or done more to help, then I would be very rich by now. People go through what I call the 'if only' stage. 'If only I had done this, said that, been there – then he/she would have been OK.' It is commonplace when we lose a loved one to think that we could have done something to prevent the death, however far-fetched this can be. But in reality, if that person was meant to die then that is it. There is nothing you could have done to prevent it, because it was fate.

The other thing that happens to people is that they feel very guilty about still being alive when their loved one has gone before them. This is particularly commonplace when the person who is grieving is older than the one who has lost their life. You must remind yourself that life doesn't work this way. It would be a better world if the old went before the young, but life isn't like that, and it isn't your fault that they have been chosen and you have been left here.

Inertia

Many people tell me that after the loss of a loved one they simply want to 'give up', to lie in bed all day and not have to confront anything that is going on around them. They appear to be listless and dead inside. They have no interest in anything outside their world, no enthusiasm and no energy. And this is completely understandable.

Sometimes we underestimate how exhausting the grieving process can be. It can drain us emotionally and physically to such an extent that we are left with no energy for anything else in our lives. All we want to do is lie around and forget about the world around us. Whilst this is understandable, we have to move on not least because this is what our loved ones in spirit want. What I advise people in this phase to do is to take life one day at a time. Each day set yourself a challenge, no matter how small it is. Try and do the housework, or go to the shops, or do your hair, or make some phone calls. And every day build on this, just one step at a time, until you feel that you can cope with living again.

Isolation

Many people tell me that their grief makes them feel isolated from those around them. They feel that they can no longer relate to people because of what has happened. You must remember that people *are* there for you, but you must also realize that they might be scared of crowding you. If you need people around you then just ask. If you cannot face talking about what has happened, then just say this to them. They will understand.

Some people get very embarrassed about death, so rather than talking to you about it they will be shy and may even avoid telephoning you or coming up to you in the street. You must make it clear to people that they can speak to you and that you would like that, but that you may not be ready to talk about your loss.

Missing people

People who 'lose' their loved ones when they go missing also grieve. If someone they love disappears, for whatever reason, these people mourn too. They may not have a body to bury, they may not even know whether or not that person is dead, but they still mourn their absence. This is probably one of the worst things that can happen to people. They never want to give up hope, they always want to believe that one day the person will walk through their door again, they still want to believe that their missing one is alive, but as the months and years go by there is an acceptance that, whilst this person may be alive, they may not see them again. They grieve the fact that they aren't with them, they mourn their absence, but the problem is that they have no closure. They are left in limbo, not knowing how to feel.

I always feel so terribly sorry for those people who have 'lost' someone in this way. I have no advice for them. I have nothing that can make it any better. It is the most terrible waiting game, mentally, emotionally and physically exhausting. They don't want to give up hope, they wait for that moment when they hear the key in the lock, or the moment when they see them in the street. They so want to believe that they are alive, but sometimes I think it would be better if they knew that they were dead because they would have closure. Their loved one would be at peace, and so would they. But of course they can't let go if they think their loved one might be alive.

This also applies when people die but their bodies are never recovered: the ones who die out at sea, in fires or at war. One of the reasons why we have funerals is so we can say goodbye. The ceremony, whether you are religious or not, gives you closure. But in this case this doesn't happen and people have to accept that their loved ones are gone without seeing they're gone. I have so much sympathy for the people who lost friends and family in the atrocities of 11 September 2001. I think that it is very hard for them to come to terms with what they have lost, not only because of the violent way in which their loved ones perished but because they had nothing of them to say goodbye to. When this happens I think it is harder to come to terms with death, and in my experience the grieving process takes much longer.

Numbness

When we are shocked by a death we may feel listless and numb. Sometimes, once the shock has subsided, we are left feeling nothing at all. I have read for people who have lost those they loved very much and they say to me, 'Why don't I feel anything?' They seem deprived of all feeling, so much so that an outsider might be completely unaware that they have lost anyone close to them. These people wear a fixed smile, get on with their lives as though nothing has happened, or walk around in a zombie-like state. It's not that this person doesn't care, but that the pain and the reality of their loss hasn't sunk in fully. In time the numbness will subside and they will begin to go through the pain and the hurt.

Resentment

When you lose someone you love it is quite natural to feel resentful, even if you aren't normally a bitter or negative person. People whose loved ones have died young can go through a period when they feel resentful towards others. If you have lost a child, you might feel resentful towards people with children. If you are young and have lost a parent, you might feel resentful towards your friends and the relationship they have with their parents. If you have lost a soulmate, you might resent those around you who are in love and still have each other. It is quite normal to go through this stage and in my experience it never lasts that long. What you have to keep reminding yourself of is that it isn't other people's fault that your loved one has died, and if you can't cope with being around those people then take yourself out of that circle until you heal.

Sadness

This is the emotion that we most associate with grief. Sadness is something that never leaves us, no matter how long it has been since our loved one has passed. We are sad for the life that has been lost and cut short, but we are also sad for ourselves and our own loss. In the early stages of the grieving process this emotion can be very intense, but as the years go on, though it lessens, it never really leaves us and there will always be a part of our heart that never really recovers from the death of someone we love.

Shock

Shock is what we go through when we are unprepared for the death of someone we love. In many ways shock is as much a physical state as it is a mental one. It is our body and our brain's way of coping with a sudden upheaval. It can leave us speechless and unable to communicate. It may cause physical side-effects such as being unable to sleep, eat or concentrate. Shock doesn't last that long, but it gives our mind and body time to adjust to the pain that we are going to feel next.

Social problems

Even the most social of people find it difficult to cope with other people once they are grieving. People who are mourning suffer from so much hurt and pain internally that they withdraw and recoil from the world outside. These people may think that others don't understand them. They may not want to be a burden to others, or cast a shadow on other people's lives. When someone loses someone they love very much, their outlook on life changes. Often they can't cope with strangers and small talk. A simple glass of wine gives them no pleasure. They feel guilty about going to a party or a social event because they feel that they cannot, will not or should not enjoy themselves.

If you are in this position be aware of this. Don't force yourself to go to things that will frighten you or you won't enjoy. But also don't cut yourself off from the world. If you cannot cope with large numbers of people, then ring your friends and ask to see them one on one. They will want to be there for you and they will understand that you can only socialize on this level at the moment.

Suicide

Often grief can be so intense that people literally give up the will to live. 'How can I carry on when I am hurting so much?' they think. 'Wouldn't it be better to be with the one I loved than to be miserable here on earth?' I can understand why people go through this, but suicide is not the answer. If you were meant to go then you would have been taken. The fact is that no matter how much you hurt, you are here for a reason. This may be to take care of those who have been left behind – your children, your spouse, your family and friends – or because you are meant to fulfil another destiny. Either way, the time isn't right and the most important thing to realize is that your spirit doesn't need you. They know that you will be reunited one day and they want you to carry on.

A LOSS OF FAITH

It is quite common to lose your religious faith when you lose a loved one. The question people most often ask me when they have suffered a tragedy is, 'If there is a God then why did He do this to me?' Of course it is quite understandable, even with the most religious of people. A couple of years ago I read for a vicar who had lost his teenage daughter and was so distraught that he felt like turning his back on the Church. How can we believe in a God who causes us so much pain? I think that if we stopped seeing death as a punishment and started to accept it for what it is – a reward – then we might be able to reconcile our beliefs with our loss. Of course it is difficult to see it this way when you are shocked by a death.

The following case history is that of a lovely Irish woman called Anne. Anne was a devout Catholic who went to church every day, but who when her beloved twins were killed turned her back on the Church. Here she tells her story:

Anne's story

When my fifteen-year-old twin boys, Cian and Gavin, died I felt like my life was over. They really were the most special boys, so full of energy and life and kindness and I wondered how my husband Vince and my other children, Lisa, Gary and my youngest Sarah, who was only ten at the time, would cope without them in our lives. Cian and Gavin had been killed in a car accident along with their best friend Connor. They had been driving with a group of young friends and their car had crashed into another vehicle. No one survived the accident.

I am a Catholic but my faith brought me little comfort after the accident. I had gone to mass every single day at seven-thirty with my boys when they had been alive. But now they were gone and praying didn't help me.

I knew about Rita Rogers because I read her column in Bella magazine. At the end of the page the magazine invites readers to write in to Rita. 'Could it be your turn next?' it asks the readers each week. Well, to be honest I very much doubted that it would be but my sister wrote in to Rita and by some kind of strange miracle within weeks we had a reply and a reading booked. I would like to say that it felt like winning the Lotto but it meant so much more than that.

The day of the reading I had the strongest sensation that my boys were with me. It started as just a feeling but as the day progressed it got more and more intense till the point where I could actually feel them pulling and tugging at me, this way and that, the way they used to do when they were excited about something.

I had asked my family to join me for the reading. Vince and Gary didn't sit in with us because it was too much for them and I think they weren't ready for it, but the rest of us were there – the boys' nana, my daughters Sarah and Lisa, my sisters Caly and Margaret. When the reading began and I started to talk to Rita she told me that I was there with my family and said that the boys were saying who was there. Not only did she tell me the names of everyone in the room but she also gave me the exact order of where they were sitting in the room.

The day of the reading I had spent some time alone. I went to the graves and had gone to the boys' bedroom and was talking to them in my mind. I asked them and their friend Connor to tell me something during the reading with Rita to prove to me that I was talking to them. If Rita didn't mention these things during the reading well then I would know she wasn't communicating with them, I figured. You see I had never been to a medium before, and whilst I was fascinated by Rita's column I had to know this was real, I had to believe.

So I asked each of the boys a personal question. 'Connor,' I said, starting with the boys' friend. 'Connor, say something to me that will make your mother happy. Tell me something that will only make sense to you and her.'

Then I asked Cian to tell me the names of my best friends who had died years ago. Martin and Tony had been my cousins as well as my close friends. The question was obscure, not something someone might know or guess, but I knew Cian knew the answer. 'Tell me the name of my cousin who drowned and the name of the one who was killed in a fire,' I asked him. Before the accident Gavin had been on at me about buying him a new pair of runners. He never asked for anything he didn't need. He was by no means a spoilt or greedy child. But for some reason I never got round to it. It wasn't that I was short of money – I am not sure why I didn't. But Gavin had been on at me every day, and so when he died I felt so guilty about this. So I sat on his bed and said to him, 'I'm sorry I didn't buy your runners,' and asked him to forgive me.

Rita told us so many things in the reading which were so accurate and true. She knew my father was sick, for example, the names of relatives who had passed away and a lot of details about our family history which I could not believe I was hearing. She said that the boys were talking to her all at once, which was typical of them for they never drew breath, and that they were saying that they were the 'three musketeers'. Well, this is how Connor and the twins always described themselves. She talked me through exactly what had happened when the car crashed, precisely where they were on the road, that they had been driving too fast and had lost control of the car. She said that Paul, the young man who had been driving the car at the time, was very, very sorry.

But it was when Rita answered my three personal questions that I then knew for sure that I was talking to my boys. 'Cian says he is here with Martin,' Rita said quite casually, 'and Anthony is there with them too.' Then she said right out of the blue, 'Gavin says you must stop worrying about his runners.' But it was Connor's message that was perhaps the most surprising of all. Rita said that Connor was telling her the name Pascal and that he was spelling it out to her. Well, I knew no one of that name and wondered whether it would mean anything to Connor's mother, Mary. I hoped and prayed it did for her sake but was very worried in case it didn't. But when I put the message to Mary later she went white. It turned out that she didn't know anyone called Pascal but the word was significant for another reason – it was her secret password for her office computer!

Rita said to me during the reading that the boys kept saying that they knew her and they were excited about this. What Rita didn't know was that the boys loved Rita's column in Bella and had always been fascinated by it. Even at the time I had been surprised by this. Why would two fifteen-year-old boys be interested in such things? But now it sort of makes sense to me and I think that they were completely instrumental in getting me a reading with Rita so quickly.

Cian and Gavin were such special children. They were different in so many ways. They were always so kind, so giving and so full of love. They never asked for anything and always put others first. It was always 'Mum this' and 'Mum that', they wouldn't argue with you about anything, they loved life and were just so full of it. They were also inseparable, they wouldn't go anywhere without each other, not even on the bus to school. And I think that in many ways knowing that they both have got each other now brings me a great *deal of comfort. I may sound like a bad mother for saying this, but if Our Lady had appeared to me and said you must choose one of them to stay and one to go, then I would have begged her to take them both. You just couldn't split them up, so the fact that they have each other now makes me happy.*

To say that the reading brought me comfort isn't enough. The reading gave me my life back. I have said that my faith brought me no comfort after the accident. To be honest, at that time I was so angry with God and so raw that if I had gone into a church and seen a statue of Jesus I may have taken a hammer to it. I couldn't understand why God would do this to me. But the reading changed that. Knowing that my boys were happy and safe in the afterlife gave me my faith back. I can now look forward, I believe in God and I have hope, and I know deep inside of me that they are happier where they are now.

ACCEPTANCE

A crucial part of the grieving process is acceptance. Until you learn to accept your loss you cannot move on and learn to live again. When I talk about acceptance I am talking not just about accepting that loss, but about accepting everything that goes with it: the pain, the emptiness, your emotions, the fact that your life will never be the same again. When you accept a death it doesn't mean that you no longer care about that person or that they are lost to you. On the contrary, what you are saying is that this terrible, terrible tragedy has happened but you have to accept that as part of your life. And when you do get to that stage, rather than feel sorry for yourself and what you have lost, you can move forward to the point where you can rejoice in what you had and the person you knew and loved.

The next story is a remarkable tale of acceptance by a very brave woman called Claudia. Claudia lost her daughter Bridie when she drowned off the coast of Australia. Claudia coped amazingly well. At the time of writing Bridie has only been gone for five months and yet Claudia has already showed great determination not only to understand her own pain but also in deciding that with her husband she will set up a bereavement refuge for other people who are suffering like they are. This is her story:

Claudia's story

Bridie was a beautiful child, quiet, creative, assertive and also quite spiritual. For a nine-year-old Bridie seemed wise beyond her years, she was always asking questions and wasn't really interested in things other little girls her age were into.

Earlier in the week a good friend of mine called Susan rang and asked whether she might be able to have my girls over to play with hers that weekend. Susan had girls the same age as ours and her kids had been over to our place to play the weekend before. So it was arranged that Bridie and her younger sister Jade, who was seven at the time, would go over to Susan's at 1 o'clock on Saturday 16 February 2002, and that my husband, who was looking after our three-year-old, Tilley, would collect them later on. That afternoon Susan decided to take the girls to the beach. She must have got there at around five-thirty. Every Saturday night we always had a 'family night' where my husband and I would make sure that we sat down for dinner with the girls. Usually we would have a Chinese takeaway. The restaurant we go to isn't far from Susan's so my husband had planned to pick up the girls on the way home from collecting the food. At around five-thirty he drove to the house but Susan and the kids weren't there. Thinking this was odd and wanting to get the girls home in time for dinner he drove to the beach to see if they were still there. When he arrived at the beach the police and the coastguard were already there and a massive search was under way. He was told that there had been two fatalities – that two bodies had been recovered from the sea but that one child was suspected as missing.

Of course we will never know precisely what happened that afternoon but piecing together what evidence we do have we know that in the late afternoon Susan and the children had gone to the beach and were playing on a sandbar which was raised above a gully of water. Susan was supervizing the kids but was on her own. The next thing we know is that somehow the sandbar gave way and her daughter Meg fell into the sea, followed by Bridie. Susan had her other daughters and Jade with her. What we know is that she went in to get Meg and managed to pull her out of the sea and get her to safety. She then went back for Bridie, but she went in with her youngest, Ally, on her hip. Bridie must have been pulled out quite far by now, and Susan with a young child on her hip must have struggled to get her, but it was too late. The bodies of Susan and Ally were recovered but we never saw Bridie again.

It's strange how life can just change so dramatically in a flash. One moment there you are, a normal person doing normal things without anything to complain about. You have a lovely life, three lovely children, a husband and you are doing normal things families do like planning Saturday night dinners. You wake up one morning, send your children out to play like you do, and then one afternoon they don't come back. And that's it. Your world and your life as you knew it isn't the same any more and never will be for the rest of your life. I was devastated. I still am.

What made things worse for us too was that Bridie's body wasn't recovered. We had to accept that she was gone and that she wasn't coming back, but that is very hard to do if your child is still 'missing'. It's hard to give up hope and to face things as they are.

Six weeks after the accident we had a reading with Rita. The reading itself was amazing and Bridie's personality came straight through. Rita picked up on so many things Bridie was about – she mentioned her favourite food (McDonald's, of course!) and other little details, but it was more about her mannerisms and the way she spoke. She talked about relatives she was with in spirit and about things that were going on at home too.

Rita also took us through the accident. None of this had been in my letter to her and frankly, given the fact that we live in Australia and she lives in England, there is no way she could have found out about any of it from anyone else. But there she was firing off the facts, bang, bang, bang, one after another. She told us about the lighthouse on the beach, the sandbar which had given way beneath their feet and how one of the little girls had fallen in first. She said that this girl she was picking up was called Megan, and that she made a point of saying that she had been christened that. I didn't know that Meg was christened Megan, to me she had always been Meg, but when I asked afterwards, sure enough, that was her real name.

I have always fervently believed in an afterlife and there was no doubt in my mind that when Bridie died she was there, but listening to Rita during the reading was amazing because it was like having a direct phone line to my daughter in heaven.

But as a mother who has lost a child, I have to be very honest about it – as good as a reading is, nothing is ever good enough. I had been so excited the week before the reading. Even though throughout the reading I was totally amazed by everything I heard, I was left wanting more. Don't get me wrong, I am not saying it didn't bring me comfort. On the contrary, it was so good that I wish I could speak to Rita every week. But part of grieving is learning to accept, and for us that means learning to accept that Bridie isn't coming back to us and learning to live without her. When I say the reading wasn't enough, I mean that nothing comes close to actually having your child with you. Nothing can or will replace Bridie and that's the sentence I will have to learn to live with.

Part of the grieving process is about acceptance. It's only been a short while since the accident and we are still very much trying to come to terms with our loss. And as young parents of young children we have to learn to rebuild our lives for the sake of our other children, but that isn't easy. For the rest of my life I now face this reality and I know that however much I recover there will always be this sadness inside of me, that every time I have a moment when I am able to enjoy myself, when I am free to let go, to have a glass of wine, there will always be this little bit of me that is terribly sad inside. And that is the unfortunate fact about death.

What Rita has helped me to understand is that Bridie's death was preordained, and that there was nothing that I could have done to prevent it. Bridie was an under-eight Nipper Champion, which *meant that she was not only a good swimmer but she knew a great deal about sea and beach safety. What happened on the beach that afternoon was beyond my control. You can't stop a child going to play with a friend you know and trust. You can't be with them every moment of their day, and if you are, who is to say something won't happen then. For some reason Bridie wasn't supposed to be with us long and I have to get used to that. In a strange way I think I had some kind of inkling, on a subconscious level, that this was going to happen. Some weeks before Bridie went I wasn't feeling myself and was suffering from insomnia. I was also doing a series of paintings, one of which was a large mural for a wall at our house. The painting is of a mermaid. She is lying on the ocean floor asleep with her tail stuck under the rocks, with a turbulent sea above her. I don't know why I painted it at the time. I just did, and now it has a degree of poignancy for me.*

Rita said at the end of the conversation that my husband and I were thinking of buying a plot of land, which we were. We were thinking of buying a place where we could set up a spiritual healing centre, a place where people could go to find some comfort for their pain and relief from their suffering. We are still heading towards that plan and hopefully one day we will be able to achieve it and help people, in much the same way that Rita was able to help us.

3. Losing a Young Child

My mother lost her first child. The baby, a daughter called Mary, was stillborn. The terrible grief and pain my mother suffered was compounded further by the fact that the baby had been conceived out of wedlock. Back in those days it was socially unacceptable to bring a child into the world if you weren't wed and so my father did the right thing by my mother and they were married. It was, then, a cruel irony and fate that the child they had built their lives around should be taken from them at that stage. Neither of them ever recovered from the loss.

My father said that little Mary had been 'too beautiful for this world'. Like me, she had inherited my grandmother's dark Romany looks – her hair shone blue because it was so black and, according to my mother, she had the face of an angel.

I have often wondered what they must have felt as they held her in her blanket. The tiny child they had just borne into this world would days later have to be buried. How hard must it have been for my mother not to hear her child's first cry moments after she had given birth? How painful was it for my father to hand his firstborn back to the nurses knowing that he wouldn't see his beloved daughter again? They dressed Mary in pink on the day she was buried and held a proper funeral for her. Though they hadn't known her for long she had changed their world, and her death cast a shadow over their lives. And despite the fact that they went on to have another six children, as far as they were concerned there would always be an empty chair at our table.

We should never have to bury the ones we have borne. We may lose our loved ones, parents, best friends, our soulmates, but whilst this grief can be unbearable it cannot compare to the utter, unthinkable pain that parents suffer when they lose their child. I have always said that losing a child is the greatest pain of all. Nothing can come close to the sheer agony suffered by a family who have had to bury one of their young. To be pre-deceased by your child is one of the most painful and distressing things in human experience.

The reason why this pain is so intense is because losing a child breaks the natural order of things. As parents we instinct-ively believe that when we bring a child into this world they will outlive us. When we bring a child into this world we do all that is humanly possible to care for them. Whether we have planned for them or not, once that baby is in our arms it is our natural instinct to put our child's needs before our own, to love, nurture and protect them. As parents we make huge sacrifices to ensure their well-being. We provide for our young emotionally, spiritually, physically and financially. Suddenly the world is no longer just about us but about the little thing we have brought into it, and we plan our, and their, future accordingly. So when a child is taken from us we feel that they have gone 'before their time'.

The death of a child is always tragic. The sight of a tiny coffin being carried to the grave, the thought of a healthy teenager's life being suddenly over or a young person being told they only have months left to live is enough to break anyone's heart. Stories in the newspapers or on the television news about children dying fill us *all* with grief and sadness. These stories touch us all whether we have children or not, because we hate to think of young lives being over before their prime and we feel a deep sense of sympathy and compassion for their family. 'I cannot begin to think what they are going through right now,' we say, not realizing how true this is, for unless you have actually lost a child yourself, you cannot begin to understand the magnitude and intensity of this kind of pain. It is a grief so strong that it almost defies description. It is one so intense that it doesn't just turn our lives upside down, it can destroy our lives, because when we lose a child we lose part of ourselves as well. When we bury our young we bury part of our soul with them.

In my experience, people who lose a child never really recover. That may sound pessimistic, but it is true. We may learn to live with the pain, to cope with it, even to put on a brave face, but the hurt that comes with that loss doesn't ever leave us. Time doesn't heal, because as any grieving parent will tell you, not a day passes when you don't think of that child. Forty years on from losing a baby you will wonder what he or she would have become if they were with you now. Each birthday or anniversary that you mark will be just as poignant and significant for you as the years pass.

Mourning a child is very different from mourning an adult whom we have loved very much. In my life I have lost a great many people I was very close to – my mother, my husband, my Romany grandmother whom I adored and many close dear friends. Even though I have always believed in the afterlife, and through my work have been in the fortunate position to be given the positive proof that there is a spirit world, each of these passings has weighed heavily on my heart. I have mourned the loss of each of them, grieved terribly and missed them. But adults who pass over have 'had their lives'. However much we miss them, they have had their experiences and 'lived'. When a child is taken from us we feel as though they have been cheated out of life. We mourn not just their death but the life they could have had if they had grown up.

Through my years of experience reading for people who have lost a child I have come to understand just how terrible this grief can be. It is a heartache that can never be healed, a loss that never leaves you, a pain that you feel physically. Across the walls of the area in which I work are hundreds of photographs of children. Small faces peer at me, tiny babies, chubby toddlers, the first school photograph, a teenager on holiday. These pictures have been sent to me by people all over the world who I have read for. The pictures are all the same – happy children enjoying life. But all of these children have passed over. Although I am fortunate never to have lost one of my own children, I am well aware of how parents suffer when they lose their young. On average I must read for at least three people a week who have lost a child and this has given me an insight into the magnitude of suffering. It is something of a vocation for me, and one aspect of my work and gift that actually makes me feel that what I do is really worthwhile. I can't bring the children back, but I know that my readings can bring their parents hope and comfort.

It doesn't matter whether you lose your child within the first year of their life, whether they have been with you for only a few days, or even if you have lost them before you bear them into this world – the pain and the grief that you suffer is as great as if you had known them for as long as a normal lifetime. The point is that the child, however young they were when they passed over, was *yours*. They were destined to be with you. You gave them life, they grew within you. (Even if you had adopted them, they were still destined for whatever reason to be yours.) From the moment that the child was conceived it became part of you, and it was at that moment that a new soul was born. Most people believe that children come into the world when they leave the mother's womb, but, as a Romany, I believe that our children are 'born' at conception because that is when life begins. We feel our children growing within us from the first bout of morning sickness to its first kick. Within seconds of that child's conception we are forging a link that will stay with us for ever. And whilst the bond between mother and child is particularly strong, that doesn't mean that the father of the child doesn't feel that connection too – remember that half of that child came from its father.

So, even if you lose a child before it has been born into this world, that loss can be extremely painful. Miscarriage is, of course, nature's way of sparing a child pain. We talk about children 'not being right for this world', and I think this is very appropriate when we are talking about miscarriage. It isn't that your child wasn't good enough for this world, it's that your baby wouldn't have been very happy in this world. It might not have been strong enough, and so that child was taken back into the spirit world to be loved, cared for and raised. You might wish that it could be there with you, but would you really want to subject it to a life of suffering and pain here when it could be happy and healthy in spirit?

Many people often underestimate the pain that miscarriage can cause parents. In pregnancy we have so much hope, so many expectations. From the moment we realize we are pregnant we start looking into our child's future. We imagine what effect this child will have on our lives, what it will look like, whether it will be a boy or a girl. We think about it in years to come, walking and talking, playing outside, going to school for the first time. We wonder what he or she will be when they grow up. You may not have started to decorate the nursery or bought a crib, but in your mind you have already started to make a place for that child in your lives, in this world. So when you lose that baby you lose all hope and promise too.

People don't really understand what parents who lose a baby at this stage are going through. Because there is no body, no coffin, no funeral, people don't think of that baby as a child. They don't really understand that you have lost a life. So what if you hadn't held your baby in your arms, nursed it or baptized it – that is irrelevant. That baby was within you, and it was very much a little person. When we lose a child in the middle of a pregnancy we feel its death. The feelings of grief can be just as intense.

In my experience, people who suffer miscarriages tend to get quite depressed not at the time of the loss but some months later. One of the reasons for this is because they haven't allowed themselves to mourn their child. Because they haven't seen their child, haven't buried it or even given it a name they don't have the closure that parents of born children have. My advice to anyone who has suffered a miscarriage is not to be ashamed or frightened to face this grief. You have just lost a child. The love you felt for that baby is just as strong as if it had been born into the world. And of course this also applies to people who have lost a child through abortion. Just because someone selects to terminate the life of their child, for whatever reason, does not mean that they do not grieve that baby's life. I cannot tell you how many times I have read for women, and men for that matter, who have mourned the loss of their child after a termination. I think that sometimes people aren't really fully aware of how they will feel following a termination. Even if they think that they are equipped to deal with the idea, many people suffer later on from very strong feelings, not just of guilt or regret but grief too.

I do not judge anyone who decides to have a termination. I know this will annoy Pro Life campaigners but – while I believe life starts at conception and is sacred – I do believe there are some children who are not meant to be here. I would rather feel a baby has gone straight to the spirit world where it will be loved and cared for, than to live a life down here where it might suffer or not be wanted. Any parent who has been in this awful position should know that their baby is safe and well in spirit and that when you die you will be reunited with your child.

The point I am making here is that no matter how long our child is with us, we have a special bond with them and it is incredibly hard for us when we lose them. Think of the mother who suffers the tragedy of a stillbirth. Imagine her pain as she has to give birth to a child she will never hear cry. As she holds that baby in her arms and says goodbye, her pain is just as strong and intense as it would be had her baby lived outside the womb. The baby may never have breathed in this world but it was still her child and she and its father will mourn the loss till their dying day. You see, it doesn't matter how long we have known our children when they are taken from us. Few people in Britain could have failed to be moved by the tragic death of Gordon and Sarah Brown's baby in January 2002. The normally dour-looking Chancellor of the Exchequer looked so ecstatic when he announced the birth of his daughter Jennifer Jane to the press waiting outside the hospital. His smile beamed from ear to ear, he could barely contain his joy. Politics aside, you could not help but warm to him – he looked so happy, he was a different man. And this is what children do to us. They melt our hearts as soon as we see them.

How cruel and tragic it was then that this child should be taken from these people just days later? I, like so many people around the country, felt terribly sorry for them and wondered how they would cope with their awful loss. But then Gordon Brown released a statement. Standing outside the hospital he said that little Jennifer Jane in her short life had touched their hearts and changed their lives for ever. It was such a simple statement to make, but so poignant. That child, but ten days old, had changed their lives for ever, and as much as they were and are to suffer through this tragedy, I think both of them know that they were blessed to have shared even that short amount of time with their precious baby daughter.

You see, each little life we bring into this world is so, so special. Our children might die when they are tiny, when they are toddlers, when they are four years old, or when they have just reached their ninth birthday. Whatever age they are, however long we have known them, it doesn't matter. Their death is devastating and leaves the most terrible hole in our lives.

ANGELS

The first question I am asked by parents who have lost a child is 'Why?' One simple word which is imbued with so much hurt, suffering and pain. The loss of a child never seems to make sense to any of us, let alone the parent. When a child has so much to live for and has brought so much joy and love into this world, is it not the greatest tragedy that their life is cut short? We can't understand why this has happened, why fate has been so cruel. Why has this child been deprived of a long and full life? Why were they punished in this way? Why, if there were a God, would He want to take our children away from us? So many terrible questions and never an answer that will satisfy.

The first thing we have to come to understand is that death is not a punishment. Even if we are religious and believe in life after death, it is hard for us to accept at times like this that the afterlife is a better place than this. As parents we instinctively feel that our children should be with us here on earth and not somewhere else. We all die eventually, and in death we are given the gift of eternal life, a chance to enter an afterlife which is free from pain, unhappiness and evil. If we come to believe in an afterlife and understand that that place is full of love and joy and peace, we might begin to view death not as a punishment but as a reward. We are all put on this earth for a reason and once we have fulfilled that role it is no longer necessary for us to remain here. Our lives are fated: we are all living out our destiny here and, as difficult as it may be to understand this, *some people are meant to die young.*

I said in Chapter One that when we go to the afterlife we begin a journey towards spiritual perfection. I believe there are some people who have already begun that journey here on earth. I am not saying that they are without sin, but there is an inherent goodness and kindness in these people that makes them incredibly special. These are the people I like to think of as angels. Of course they don't have wings, haloes and harps! But there is something about these people that sets them apart from the rest of us. They are not just special, they are quite exceptional. They are the ones who overflow with love, the ones who always put others first, who bring us joy just by walking into a room and radiate happiness wherever they go, whatever they do. And I believe that these people were sent here for that reason. To bring light and warmth into a world that can be so dark and cold at times.

When I talk to parents who have lost a child they *always* say the same thing to me: my child was so special. 'I'm not just saying this, but he *really was* special,' they will say. Or 'I can't put my finger on it, but there was something about her that just made everyone so happy and love her so much.' When people say this to me I don't doubt for an instant that their child wasn't special. These parents are not romanticizing the memory of their child, their child really *was* like this. I believe these children are sent to us to help us, to enrich our lives, to bring us hope and to make us happy. Not only do they touch our lives, they actually make our world a better place – like the five-year-old terminally sick boy who knows he hasn't got long here and teaches his doctors and parents a thing or two about bravery, the nine-month-old baby girl who, through her smile and aura, shows her parents just how deep love can be, the seven-year-old boy with leukaemia who still dreams of playing for England and fashions what's left of his hair into a David Beckham mohican. Each of these children is special. They show us a depth of courage, love, hope and determination that we as adults had never known before, that we didn't think was possible.

These little people, and older children too, come into our world for a short time and change our lives for ever. They have such a profound effect on us that their loss is almost too much to bear. How can we carry on without them, we ask.

Well, the first thing to understand is that their life here, however brief it was, was a blessing. I know it is hard to do, but rather than mourn their death and your loss, celebrate their life and what you gained from them. Don't think how unlucky you are for losing them, think how lucky you were for having them here in the first place. I believe that these special children are lent to us by the spirit world. They come into our lives to help us and bring us love. They enlighten us spiritually, love us physically, show us compassion, and bring us joy and peace. And this is why I describe them as angels, because they come here and do God's work and spread his message. Of course no one is perfect and they were human, they may have been naughty at times, dis-obeyed you or been mischievous, but in essence they were good, loving children. And the fact that they brought so much to your life is why you suffer so much when they go. As I keep saying, grief comes from love. The more you love, the greater the loss. And because we have unlimited unconditional love for our children, that grief becomes unbearable.

When you think of the child who has passed away, think not of the long days and years that lie ahead without them, think of the days you shared together when you had them here with you. Think of that moment when they first smiled at you from their cradle and what joy you felt when they said their first words. Think of the unconditional love they gave you, the presents they made you, their first school play. Remember the kindness they showed to others, their love for their pets and favourite toy, the moments that made you proud. And think of what they taught you about life and how they changed your world. You will never get over the pain of losing your child, but you will learn to live with it, and when you look at your child's life in this way you will come to understand that your child was a gift you were given, albeit for a very short time.

SPIRIT CHILDREN

Spirit children like to spend a great deal of time with us here on earth. The readings I give parents who have lost a child are always incredibly rich in detail. Quite often I don't have a clue what the children in spirit are talking about during the readings, but whilst these details about their toys, friends, PlayStations, favourite cuddly toys and pets mean nothing to me, they mean a great deal to their families. Recently I read for a mother who had lost her little girl. She was just short of her fifth birthday when she passed away. During the reading I kept getting the name Emily over and over again, but I couldn't put it to a person. I wasn't picking up anyone in spirit with that name and I didn't feel that it was the name of anyone the mother knew who was living. Eventually I asked the mother what the significance of the name was. 'Emily?' she asked, and then she laughed. 'That was her favourite name, in fact she liked it so much she called all her dolls by the same name.'

Spirit children like to spend a great deal of time here visiting their families because they miss them and like to be around them. Parents who have lost children often say to me that they can sense their children around them. They ask me if they might be imagining it or dreaming it because they so want it to be true. I always say to people when they ask me this that if they really felt that their child was there then they probably were. I don't say this to placate them, I say it because their child probably was there with them. The reason why I can say this with such confidence is that during a reading spirit children always give so much proof that they have been with their families. They know when you have made a change in the house, what their brothers and sisters or friends are up to, that you are thinking of buying a dog, or having another child. The details are extremely specific and, as parents always say to me, are not things that I could have guessed or made up.

You will know when they come to you because you will feel an immense feeling of love around you. You might feel a slight breeze, or feel that someone is gently blowing on you. One mother I read for says that she feels her daughter run her fingers through her hair, just as she used to do when she was alive. Another mother says that she can always tell when her son comes to her because he always plays with the light switches or turns the radio up to get her attention. One father I read for says that every time his son visits them the family dog gets very excited and starts barking and wagging his tale furiously just as he did when he saw the boy when he was alive. If you have lost a child and wonder whether they come to you, look out for these little signs.

When people lose a child, one of the primary concerns is how they are now. Parents often worry about their children being cold or lonely. They don't like to think of them in the grave or being in pain and so they always ask me at the beginning of the reading whether they are OK. If you have lost a child or know someone who has, the first thing to understand is that no matter how your child died, whatever pain or suffering they had to endure at the time of their death they are now fine, well, happy and safe in spirit. They aren't lying there cold or lonely in their grave, because they have already ascended into the spirit world and they did this long before they were buried. When they died they would have immediately passed over into the spirit world and they would have been fetched by someone you know who is in spirit. If you don't know anyone well who has passed over then your child would have been fetched by one of your guardian angels.

Your child wouldn't have been in pain because there is no pain in spirit. Once they had passed over they would have felt fit and healthy again. Had they suffered from illness in this life, had they been in any way disabled, they wouldn't carry it to the spirit world because we are all perfect in spirit. Had they been frightened at the time of their death they wouldn't feel that in spirit. There is no fear in the spirit world, and no harm can come to anyone there. When a child ascends into the spirit world they are well looked after and deeply loved. They are free to travel and visit us here and they can spend as much time as they want here on the earth plane. But the most important thing to know is that your child in spirit is happy and well and will be reunited with you on the day that you pass over.

Ashley's and Elaine's story

The story that follows involves two mothers, Ashley and Elaine, who are great friends. They met at an antenatal class when they were both preparing to have their first children. They became firm friends and that bond was to become stronger still when they both gave birth to boys. Over the next few years Elaine and Ashley and their sons Mitchell and Elliot and then their second children spent a great deal of time together. Given that they had so much in common it was no wonder that they became so close. Ashley and Elaine were young women, both married, both with two young boys, and they got on so well together that not only did they spend a lot of time together as the boys played, but they even went on holiday together.

But then suddenly something tragic happened. Ashley's son Elliot drowned and things were never the same again. Elaine was a great support to Ashley and tried to help her get through this awful time, but as any parent who has lost a child will say, you never really know that kind of pain until you have been through it yourself. How tragic, how ironic and how cruel it then was that within three years of this happening Elaine's own son Mitchell would be dead too.

Here they tell their own remarkable and sad stories:

Ashley:

My husband Toni and I were invited on holiday to stay in a villa in Spain with my in-laws and our children. It was to be our first holiday in ages and given the fact that the villa had a pool and it was summer, normally I would have been thrilled by the prospect of two weeks of sun, rest and time with my family. But right from the start I wasn't happy about the idea. I don't know why, maybe it was intuition, but there was something holding me back, telling me not to go. No one would have understood this; I couldn't have explained it and so we went. If only we hadn't.

The villa was lovely, the weather was great and the children were having a wonderful time. They loved the freedom of being able to run around and they loved swimming in the pool. The four of us adults were well aware of the attractions of a swimming pool for young children and so we were religiously vigilant about keeping watch on the children and also the pool area. There wasn't a moment when someone wasn't watching out for them, or so we thought.

It must have happened within a window of not more than ten minutes. I'm not really sure what did happen, it was all so quick, so panicked and confused. I have real trouble remembering that day as it is. But what I can remember is asking someone where Elliot was and them saying 'I thought he was with you'. That was it – we all looked at each other and started to search. Someone went to the pool but he wasn't there and so we called out, searched the villa and the garden. It was a very sunny day. The sun reflecting on the pool was almost blinding but a quarter of it was in the shade. That's where we found him. When we had checked the pool minutes before we must have missed him because of the shade. We gave him mouth to mouth, again and again. We called the medical team and they tried again. But it was too late.

Elliot was the most enchanting child. He was four years and four months old when he went. And I have to say that he had both of us round his little finger. It wasn't just that he was our firstborn, although that does put children in a special part of your heart, it was that he was very special. He wasn't naughty, but he had this wonderful mischievous streak in him, you know the way little boys should. He had this look about him, this way of really getting to you, and everyone who knew him completely adored him. He was so full of energy and charm but he was also a very loving child.

The days that followed were a living nightmare. We were stuck in a foreign country not knowing what to do, and we couldn't get home until it had all been sorted out for us to return to England with Elliot's body. I took a lot of drugs to get me through those days. I was in shock. I felt numb, devastated, hurt – I didn't know how to react or behave. I wasn't prepared for this.

When I got back to England I was given a copy of one of Rita Rogers's books. It was about children who had passed over and I was moved by what she said. But I have to be very honest – by this stage I was suicidal, I didn't really think that I could carry on. They put me on Prozac but it didn't do that much for me. The thing is that I missed Elliot so much I couldn't think of living without him. I was very low. Yet despite this I did believe that Elliot was somehow around me. I had experienced a series of what I call 'pleasures' when I felt him near me. My great friend Jackie had written to Rita asking for help and saying that she didn't think I would be able to make it through this time unless I spoke to someone. In the meantime I wrote too. I wasn't aware Jackie had written, I just thought that I needed to. I didn't tell Rita what had happened to Elliot but I did send a picture of him. I didn't even tell her his name. I knew from the book I had read that she didn't like too much information.

I didn't really imagine that she would get back to me but within weeks she had and an appointment was made. Although I believed in some kind of afterlife and in a notion that people don't really die as such, I was sceptical. I needed to be really sure she was talking to him. That meant so much to me. And so with this in mind I went to the reading and in my head asked Elliot to prove three things to me so I knew that it really was him. I wanted to know why his football alarm clock kept ringing. It wasn't set and I wondered if it was him. I wanted to see if he mentioned his Thomas the Tank Engine watch. This was his favourite thing and I thought that if it was him he would refer to it. And last of all I wanted to see Elliot; I wanted Rita to perform a transfiguration.

I can't tell you what it was like when each of these things happened during the reading. Rita mentioned the alarm, said it was shaped like a football and that Elliot set it off. I had taken Elliot's Thomas the Tank Engine watch with me to the reading and had kept it in my bag. Rita mentioned Thomas the Tank Engine. She said, 'Is it the books he likes?' And then she said that he was telling her he had a watch. She said it was in my bag. I pulled it out and gave it to her and she told me that 'Mitchell' had given it to him. Then she transfigured and, although I was expecting to see Elliot, it was an *amazing experience to see my mother smiling at me again. She had passed away ten years ago and this gave me great comfort and reassurance that she lived on and was now looking after Elliot for me. There was so much other information she gave me, but these were the three things that mattered most. I knew with Rita that I had my son back. She proved to me that he was there. She knew so much: how he died, the way he looked, what he liked. She hadn't any idea about what had happened. Neither Jackie nor I had told her, and yet here she was describing exactly how my son had died and what he was like.*

Rita Rogers gave me my life back, she gave me a reason to live and an understanding that Elliot was well. She kept saying in that wonderfully calm voice of hers, 'He's just fine.' And every time she spoke to him, she kept smiling, as though she really liked talking to him. I can't begin to tell you how much this reading helped me. Rita saved me. But what I didn't know at the time was that in only a short period of time she would save my friend Elaine too.

Elaine:

On the morning of 11 October 2000 the telephone rang. It was the school asking me if I could come and collect my son. They told me that Mitchell, who was six at the time, had a terrible pain in his leg and was in tears. When I arrived at the school and saw what a state Mitchell was in I picked him up and took him straight to the local hospital. I had my youngest, Peony, with me who had just turned one, but fortunately my elder daughter, Tamara, three, was at nursery. When I registered with Accident and Emergency I asked if Mitchell could be given something there and then for the pain. He was assessed quite quickly and the doctor gave him some Calpol. He said that Mitchell's leg felt hot and it was possible that he had some kind of infection. Realizing that we might be at the hospital for some time I arranged for Ashley to come and get Peony and for Tamara to be collected from nursery.

Mitchell never complained about anything so it was obvious that he was in agony. I asked if there was anything else they could give him while we waited and so he was given some morphine and was sent for an X-ray. Initially I was told that if it was an infection they could give him a course of antibiotics, but six hours later I was told that they were unhappy with the X-ray and they would like us to return the next day for an MRI scan. I was now seriously worried. The following day we returned to the hospital. My husband Andy came with us because I was worried that Mitchell would be scared of the scanner and that I would have trouble getting him in it. Mitchell was scared, and he asked if his fluffy dog, Tom, could go in with him. The man who was operating the machine was very kind and so after a while, with a little persuasion, Mitchell and Tom were coerced into the scanner.

I had to wait all day for the results but it felt longer. At 4 p.m. the doctor finally called with the news. It was devastating. I was told that my little boy had a very rare bone tumour which they were 99 per cent sure was osteosarcoma, and that he would have to be referred to the Royal National Orthopaedic Hospital in Stanmore as they couldn't treat him there. My world fell apart. As the doctor went through the details and arranged to meet us the next day I was in a state of shock and despair. All I could think was that my little boy had a tumour and how on earth was I going to tell him.

I didn't want to tell Mitchell that he had cancer, I hated that word, how do you explain that to a six-year-old child who is so sensitive and nervous. I wanted him to fight this positively, so I told him that he had bad cells in his leg and that we would have to fight off the baddies and win the battle. Andy and I knew that it was going to take quite some time for Mitchell to get better and by chance we had booked a weekend away with our friends Jackie and Michael and their children at a campsite in Dorset. Wanting to stick to our routine and spend some quality time together before Mitchell's treatment, we decided to go on the trip as planned. Jackie was a great friend, also having a boy the same age called Frankie. We had found Elliot's death very hard to deal with and although we were all still very close friends and spent a lot of time together, Ashley and Toni had not been away with us as a group because they found it very difficult to watch Mitchell and Frankie playing together without Elliot. But when Ashley heard about Mitchell she decided that they would come on the weekend too, and she was a wonderful support. We watched Mitchell play, but he was in so much pain that it filled us all with tears.

And so after that weekend our roller coaster ride began. Hospital trips, X-rays, tests. Finally it was confirmed that Mitchell did have osteosarcoma, a rare bone tumour that normally affects teenagers. The good news was that it was treatable with an 80 per cent success rate. He would have three sets of chemotherapy, an operation to remove the tumour, and then three more sets of chemo which would be done at another hospital in London. Chemotherapy was not performed at the Royal National Orthopaedic Hospital.

Taking your child for chemotherapy isn't easy. As we went round the hospital ward we were shocked to see all these little children with no hair and it suddenly hit me how hard the next six months would be, and also made me wonder how I was going to cope without being there for our other children who were so used to me *being at home. But I couldn't leave Mitchell. It was tough watching the change in Mitchell as bag after bag of chemotherapy was fed through tubes into him. My happy little boy became quiet and withdrawn and it was then that the sickness began. We left London to go back home. I couldn't get over how many pills he had been given and I was suddenly very frightened.*

Mitchell was admitted to the local hospital, which was better because his friends and family could be with him, but he wasn't well. As he had more chemo his hair fell out, but he was always very brave and so sweet. I couldn't believe that this wonderful, caring child was having to endure so much. And so it went on and on. He had the operation but could not walk on his leg for six weeks, so he was put into a wheelchair. The chemo that followed wiped him out, but still he tried to be so happy and so brave, never complaining.

We celebrated the end of his treatment with a weekend away and I suppose we all hoped that this would be the end of it all, but that weekend I noticed that Mitchell kept saying 'pardon' a lot and wanted the television on very loud. After yet more tests we were told that he had high-frequency hearing loss; a side-effect of chemotherapy. I was devastated all over again. We had him measured for a hearing aid – luckily I found a bright-coloured one with a motorbike on it. Mitchell went back to school, learning to walk again and awaiting his hearing aid. We were finally on the road to recovery I thought, but unfortunately not. He had only been back at school for a few weeks when he started to say he had no energy. He was admitted to hospital again; his leg had become infected. On top of that he had developed shingles. Following a routine check-up it was discovered he had an enlarged heart, another side-effect of chemotherapy. I couldn't believe what was happening. The problems with Mitchell's major organs terrified me. He was in a lot of pain and seemed to be giving up. I felt so helpless. Things eventually got so bad that we were sent to a heart specialist at Great Ormond Street, the children's hospital in London. We asked them if it was serious. Nothing that drugs can't cure, we were told. I can't tell you how relieved we were. These were experts from a top London hospital, they had to be right, and there must be hope.

Two days later Mitchell died suddenly in the evening from heart failure. It was 4 June 2001, eight months since he was first diagnosed. Our boy was dead. We had trusted the experts. We had been told that he was OK and that there was nothing that drugs couldn't cure, but no one had looked at the bigger picture. No one had really listened to or looked at our little boy because he just didn't want to complain or make a fuss. How tragic that a seven-year-old boy says he has had enough, that he can't cope with the pain any more and — because the doctors don't listen and we trust them — just gives up.

I was destroyed. It is hard to describe the emotions that go through you, the if onlys, whys, buts, the anger. I had always been frightened of cancer, but I never expected my child to get it. I never expected that it would be my child that would die from it, I always thought that it would be me. I couldn't believe what had happened — especially after Elliot. Our close group of friends, three families with their three little boys and now two of them had gone.

We buried Mitchell's ashes next to Elliot. Elliot's grave was next to a tree and there was a place next to him which was vacant and that's where we wanted Mitchell to be. We put him there along with many personal things — which included the motorbike hearing aid, which he had never got to wear, and Andy's watch. Andy had planned to leave this to Mitchell in his will, but now he wanted it to go with him. We got through the funeral as we had with every-thing else because we had to. But after it was over so was my life. Mitchell was my life.

People would say to me, at least Mitchell wasn't suffering any more, that he wouldn't have liked how he was. To be honest I didn't care, I was a selfish mother and I still wanted my boy, whatever condition he was in. I was prepared to nurse him for the rest of his life as long as I had him here with me. Maybe I was being selfish – but I think that anyone who has been in my position would have understood how I was feeling.

The other thing you encounter is isolation. People are there for you in the beginning, but as time goes on they have their own lives to lead. Suddenly the phone stops ringing and the visitors stop coming. They may move on, but you are stuck in a black hole you can't get out of. Your life is destroyed by your loss. People mean well but don't really know what to say. Sometimes they are better off not saying anything. You know that people avoid you because they don't know what to say, but equally you find yourself doing the same. You don't want to have to put on an act and pretend everything is OK, but you have to. And so you become a great actor. You put on a front, but really you are crying inside. You know that there are people who are worse off than you are, but still it makes no difference. You want what you haven't got – and for me that was Mitchell.

I found that my belief was challenged a lot. After seeing so many sick children suffering I don't think I had any faith left and it made me think that this must be hell. I found that I questioned myself all the time too. No matter how many people told me that I was a good mother, I couldn't help feeling that somehow I had failed. My little boy was no longer here – it was my job to look after him and protect him and I had failed. People said it would be good to get away, but as anyone knows who has been through this, you can't get away from such a loss.

And so the tables had turned. Three years ago I had been there for Ashley, now she was there for me, the difference being that when I was there for her I had no idea what she was going through. But now she did for me. When Elliot died I read books because I thought it might help Ashley, and one of the books was written by Rita. Rita had been the one who had helped Ashley and Toni but I knew that she no longer saw people and had not done for quite a while. I hadn't seen a medium before, but I needed to know that my boy was OK. I saw a couple of recommended mediums – one was quite good and accurate and the other did nothing but upset me by telling me that Mitchell was crying. Ashley knew how upset I was, and so she called Rita's secretary and asked if she would call me.

There is a very fine line, I think, between coping and not. I had thought about giving up. I thought that the girls would be fine with their father and I could be with Mitchell. I also understand now how easy it is to drown everything in alcohol. Anything to try to escape the reality of what has happened. And then Rita called.

The voice on the other end of the phone was a woman with a strong Northern accent. She introduced herself as Rita Rogers and said that she had rung to reassure me that no child in spirit was unhappy. My tears began to flow. I grabbed a pen and notepad and shut the door so I could concentrate on what she was saying. She began gently by saying that all spirit children are happy, that they are never cold, always warm and that there is someone there to take care of them. Time, she said, wouldn't heal, which is quite accurate, but she said I would get more used to the idea.

Rita hadn't called me at that point to give me a reading, she had called to make sure I was OK, to have a chat and to make an appointment for me to see her in six months' time. But then something very odd happened. Just as we were chatting she said to me, 'I feel he wasn't very old, did he pass with cancer?' I said yes. 'Was he about seven or eight?' I said yes, and told her that he was seven. 'Is he one of three?' Again, yes. And then she said, 'He's here with me right now, he was the eldest. Mummy's little soldier. He was a very brave little boy and he's saying it's time for you to be brave now.' 'He's beautiful,' she said. 'He can run and skip and jump.' I was amazed. Then she asked, 'Who's had a birthday recently?' I told her that it was Mitchell's great-grandmother, it was her eightieth, and that we had all gone out for a family meal the day before to celebrate. 'Who's Andrew?' she asked. 'His father,' I replied. 'And James?' James was a friend who was there at that moment playing on Mitchell's PlayStation. 'He knows he is playing with one of his toys. He loves you and says he is very happy. He did try to be happy. Did he have new shoes? He is telling me about shoes with lights.' I told Rita that Mitchell had been cremated in his flashing trainers. 'You should have kept them,' she said. 'It wasn't him they cremated, just his shell. He's very happy. He has found a Granddad, and a William, John/Jack and a Lee or Liam, and a Ben. He has lots of friends in spirit! He is saying there is no need for you to come, he's all right. He's a lovely little boy and he's found Ashley's boy,' she said.

She then paused. 'He's not an M, is he? He's an M, isn't he? Is he an MA or MI? Is he MIT . . . is he Mitchell?' I said yes. 'He's saying I'm Mitchell and to tell Mummy I am happy and to stop crying. He was very proud of his service. He's not crying, he is laughing and he says it's OK for James to play with his PlayStation.

Has he got a sister?' I replied yes. 'He was your only little boy wasn't he? I feel cancer all over him; it would have gone all over him. He was spared a lot of pain. He was too good for down here . . . I feel that it was less than a year.'

Rita said that though Mitchell's cancer was only in his leg he would have been riddled with it. 'Thank God they took him before. If you could see his happy smiling face you'd know he's OK. He wants you and Andy to stay here and take care of the girls. He is very happy,' she said.

I couldn't believe what Rita had told me in the reading and I felt uplifted and no longer suicidal. But six months is an awfully long time and although the conversation with Rita helped for a while, suddenly it all got to me again. It is a bit like taking a painkiller for very bad pain, and then it wears off. But still I held on to our appointment. Andy and I were going to visit her in person for the reading. Ashley and Toni were delighted about the appointment and wished us well. The day of 5 April 2002 came and I was very nervous. Rita led us into her reading room and I turned on my tape recorder.

The reading with Rita was extraordinary. As I look at over fifteen pages of typewritten transcription that I have from that day there is little that Rita didn't know about Mitchell. Once again she gave us his name, spelling out, only this time she said his second name was Thomas. We shook our heads, that wasn't right, but Rita kept getting Thomas over and over. Then she said, 'Why does he keep mentioning Thomas? He had a dog . . . he's got a dog called Tom, a soft toy. I'm making it Thomas but he calls it Tom. Oh, and he is telling me it's Mitchell and Tom, not Mitchell Thomas, he's got it there with him!'

Rita told us how he likes to go to his room a lot and look at his things. She named his sisters, getting 'Tammy' and 'Mara' for Tamara and 'Penny' or 'Piony' for Peony. She knew about the trainers with the lights. And then she said, 'I've never known a child that tells me how many things they've got with them . . . good God! He's gone with a packed suitcase,' Rita laughed. I explained to Rita about the box we had filled and buried with Mitchell. And so Rita told us that Mitchell had his trainers, his fluffy dog Tom – and Andy's watch!

She told us the names of everyone we knew in spirit, she talked about Elliot and how Mitchell and he had found each other and were happy. She named his toys, knew that we had been to a tribunal and talked a lot and in great detail about what had happened to Elliot. And she also talked to Andy and me about the effects of losing a child. She said we wouldn't get over it but we would get used to it, and it was like having some part of you ripped out. I found her words to be very true.

Rita said that he had been too good for this world and that it's always the special children that die. She kept saying that he wasn't unhappy or crying, as though she knew what that other medium had said to me. All the time it was about how happy he was and what a beautiful boy he was and that made me happy. It meant so much to me to know he was no longer suffering and that he was with Elliot too.

On the way home I called my mother to check that everything was OK with the girls. She said that they had gone to town with my sister and her two young girls and that they had all caught the bus back. On their way back the bus went over a bridge and Peony shouted, 'Look Mitchell! We are going over a bridge!' 'Where is

Mitchell?' my mother asked her. 'Over there!' she replied, pointing to an empty seat on the bus. Peony is only two and a half, she couldn't have made that up at such a young age. It's nice to know that she does see him and play with him, like Rita had told us she did during the reading. I just wish that I could do the same.

Meeting Rita and spending so much time with her makes me question why some people have so much hostility to the work she does. Rita is a kind, caring person who does so much to help bereaved people and asks for nothing in return. If what she does helps people like us get through this and still be here, what is so wrong with that? Surely it's only good? Through talking with people like Rita I have hope that my little boy is OK and will always be with me, even though I cannot see him. One day we will be together again. I owe it to him to be brave now, as he was so brave for me.

The remarkable circumstances of Elliot and Mitchell also make us think that there must be more to it all. They were not only born within two weeks of each other and brought our families together, but they both died at a young age and are now buried next to each other. I am just pleased that, as Rita says, Mitchell and Elliot are still best friends and do everything together in spirit just as they would if they were still with us here.

4. *Losing an Older Child*

I received a letter last year from a woman in Australia. She had written to the magazine *New Idea* where I had an advice column at the time and wanted me to answer a question for her: would she 'ever get over the death of her teenage daughter?' Even though I knew what the answer to this question was straight-away, I pondered over it for a while. My daughter's own ill health over that summer had made me very conscious of the special and precious relationship between mother and daughter, parent and child. Mandy had been very seriously ill and the news of her illness had come as a terrible shock for all of us.

Reading this letter brought all that home to me. Would this woman in Australia ever 'get over' the loss of her daughter (it had been five years now, and she was still in deep pain)? Well, the answer to this is no. Even though I believe in the afterlife, in a spirit world, in the notion that none of us really 'die' but just move into another world, I had to ask myself how I would feel in the same situation. How would I cope now if one of my daughters died? Not very well, is the answer. Would I get over it? Never. For you never get over the death of a loved one, particularly not your child. You can move on, learn to live with your pain, but you never get over that kind of loss.

My daughters are all adults now, all married with homes and

families of their own. And it's funny that although they are all grown up (two of them in their forties) and have husbands and children, I still always think of them and refer to them as my 'girls'. I am sure they all find this incredibly irritating at times! But the fact is that though our relationships have adjusted over the years as they have grown up and moved away, the premise of our relationships has never altered. I am their mother and they are my babies. And it will always be like that to me.

It doesn't matter how old your child is, your relationship with them doesn't really change that much. You never stop loving your child, however old they are. Naturally, as your children grow older you have to learn to adjust as you give them more space and independence. You have your highs and lows, ups and downs but the relationship between parent and child never really changes. If I lost one of my daughters now it would be as painful for me as it would be for a mother who lost her seven-year-old child. The fact that they had grown up and had a bit more of life wouldn't console me, it wouldn't ease my grief or pain. The natural order of their life would have been broken. I wouldn't want any of mine to go before me. It wouldn't be right and it would destroy me. I remember looking at photographs taken of the late Queen Mother at the funeral of her daughter Princess Margaret and feeling so terribly sorry for her. She looked so sad, so heartbroken. The knowledge that her daughter was out of pain and had lived a full life may have brought her some comfort, but it cannot have been easy for her to say goodbye to her youngest daughter. As I keep saying, we shouldn't have to bury our young, whatever age they are.

In the last chapter I talked about what it is to lose a young child. In this chapter I want to concentrate on what happens when we lose an older child. When I refer to 'older' children I am talking about children of ten and above. And by 'above' I mean of *any* age thereafter. I have made the distinction because I find we grieve the loss of an older child in a different way from that of a young child. I am not suggesting for one moment that the grief is any worse – losing a child of *any* age is a complete tragedy – but I have noticed that there are differences in the way we react to the loss and cope with the grief.

We have a different kind of relationship with our very young children than with those who have grown up. Children below the age of ten are very much still our babies. They might be going to school and have very distinctive personalities, they might seem very grown-up at times, even wise beyond their years, but to all intents and purposes they are still little babies. They depend on us as parents for everything, and as such we are the apexes of their little world. Even if they have made friends and get on well with their brothers and sisters, the most important relationship they have is with you, the parent.

But as a child gets older that relationship starts to change. By the time a child reaches double figures they are already becoming little adults. They will have started forming meaningful relationships with other children. Rather than just having friends who are simply playmates, the child will have started to 'choose' his or her friends, children they will learn to confide in, to talk to, to grow up with. They will have started to form opinions and tastes. They will look to others such as teachers, friends, even television and the media for influences. They will form interests and relationships outside the nucleus of the home and the security of their junior school. As they grow, so too does their personality. And so as parents we learn to step back and give them more and more independence so that they can find themselves and develop.

We know our child still loves us just as much as they did when they were tiny. We know they still need us. But now we have to let go slightly and allow them to be their own person. And as they grow older and into adulthood and beyond, our relationship with them becomes more complex.

During the teenage years, our relationship with our children becomes further complicated by adolescence and raging hormones. Teenagers like to think that they know it all and that we are too overprotective. They feel that we don't want them to grow up and they crave more independence. We as parents try to respect this and yet balance it with our own experience of what the world out there is really like. They may act, look and talk like adults, yet we know how vulnerable they still are. And so the relationship we have with our teenage children becomes very intense. They no longer have the blind faith in us that they had when they were very young, and we no longer have complete control over them. We may fight, argue, question our relationship – but the love we have for each other is just as strong.

As the older child becomes an adult, we as parents have to learn to sit back and watch them make their own decisions and life choices. This can be very difficult for us because we still want to guide and protect them, yet we have to give them space, even if this means watching them make mistakes, getting into trouble, being disappointed or getting hurt. It can be very difficult, but it is also very rewarding. Nothing can compare with the feelings of immense pride we have in our children when they do well. And likewise, nothing can compare with a parent's compassion when things don't go right for our offspring, because our love for our children remains unconditional.

The grief suffered by parents who lose an older child is extremely intense and also, I have found, very complex. The deep sense of pain, loss and sadness is accompanied by a whole range of other emotions such as guilt (which is extremely common and which I will talk about later), anxiety, depression, loss of faith and anger. But I have found the most common reaction to the loss of an older child is a sense of deep bewilderment. Parents who lose an older child often say to me, 'Why? Why did this happen to my child who had offered so much and still had so much to give and to live for?' I would be a very happy woman if I could find an answer that would satisfy.

Parents who lose an older child find it difficult to cope with their absence. They have spent so much time and devotion in bringing up this child by educating them, loving them, helping them develop that they feel quite lost when their child dies and literally don't know what to do with themselves. Suddenly the house seems very quiet. There is no longer the sound of their pop music blaring out from the bedroom, no one endlessly playing on a games console or computer. No one nagging you for money, to be lent the car, to stay out later. There is no one to tell to set the table, to pick up their things, to tidy their rooms and suddenly there is one less washing load to put on.

It is ironic that the things and habits that used to irritate us so much as parents when our children were alive are suddenly the things we miss the most! So many parents have said to me how much they miss their child's noise. I know a father who used to drive round in his car at the weekends so he could listen to his son's favourite radio station and listen to the music full blast. Some mothers have told me how they miss their child's mess, whilst other parents tell me how the loss of their child has just created such a terrible hole in their lives. 'You don't realize how much of your time they took up until they have gone,' writes one mother. 'One weekend you are in a car taking them from swimming to a game, to a party, staying up to make sure they come home in time, waking them up to make sure they have done their homework . . . and then the next weekend there you are with nothing to do and that's when you realize that your child really was your life. Not only have you lost your son, you have lost your life.' I find that this is a common problem for people who have lost a child and it becomes all the more acute if the child is an only one, or is the last to have left the nest. When we lose our child, we lose our responsibility. We may feel that our role as a parent is now redundant, and that can be very difficult to adjust to.

But whilst our routines may alter or stop, what I want you to remember is that your child has only *passed over*. You may not have them around you, see or hear them, but I assure you that they are very much with you. You will have to adapt and learn to fill your weekends and evenings, you will have to get used to being alone and the house being quiet, but in many respects you would have had to do this anyway when your child grew up and fled the nest. For your child, being in spirit is rather like having gone off to college or on a trip around the world. They have gone off to spread their wings, experience new things, find new worlds and you are left at home missing them. OK, so you don't get to see them in the holidays or speak to them on the telephone, but make no mistake, your child is alive, they are with you, they do visit you and they never ever stop loving you.

IF ONLY

As parents we always think that we could have done more to prevent our children from dying. This is a very natural and common emotion for a parent to go through when they have lost their child. It is instinctive to feel protective towards and responsible for our young whatever their age, and there will always be a moment when we think that we could have done more for them. But sometimes this feeling of thinking that we could have done more becomes very intense, so much so that the grieving parent becomes racked with guilt about their child's death.

In Chapter Two I explained how feelings of guilt are part and parcel of the grieving process. Now I want to focus on why parents who lose children feel in some way responsible for their deaths, even if that death was completely beyond their control. As parents we feel it's our duty to protect our children from harm, danger, anything that might hurt them. From the moment they are born we set about making their lives as secure and as safe as we possibly can. We inoculate them, look after their health, protect them from strangers and car traffic. For the first years of their lives we barely let them out of our sight.

As they get older we have to learn to let go and give them more independence. We have to allow them to stand on their own two feet. We have to allow them the freedom to make their own decisions and choices and the physical space in which to grow. This is a very difficult part of parenthood. We want what is best for our children at all times, but we know we cannot always be there for them and so we have to learn to trust both them and, more importantly, ourselves. The parent has to decide how much freedom the child may have and has to have faith in that decision. Letting go is hard, but as I say, it is part of growing up and parenting.

The problem is, what happens when we let go and give our children freedom but that backfires? Too often I have read for parents who have lost an older child and torment themselves with the fact that they should have and could have done more to prevent that death. They go through the 'if only's. If only I hadn't let him walk to school on his own, cross that road, take the school trip, go swimming. If only she hadn't taken the bus, gone on that year off, learned to drive, borrowed my car, gone with that boy, gone to that party and so on. These parents literally begin to beat themselves up over this. They rock back and forth, clench their fists till they draw blood, pull at their hair in clumps, berating themselves for having killed their child. Even in cases where the child has passed from a terminal illness or fatal disease you see these parents blaming themselves. It was my fault she got that bug, my genes with the problem, my fault it wasn't diagnosed in time.

Throughout this book I speak about fate and destiny, and in the previous chapter I discussed how I believe that there are some people who are just not meant to spend a normal lifetime on this earth plane. I described them as angels. The idea that there are some people who are too special and too good for this world doesn't apply just to very young children but to children of all ages. Ask any parent who has lost an older child, teenager or someone in their twenties or thirties and you will be told how special and exceptional they were. The fact is that God didn't want your child to spend too much time on this earth, and so it was that your child's death was predetermined by a greater force. Whether they passed in an accident, as a result of a long illness or sudden disease, your child was meant to go, and there is nothing you could have done to stop that from happening.

Only recently I read for a woman who had lost her son. He had just completed his master's degree. This boy was an absolute genius who was looking forward to a brilliant career in academia. To celebrate his achievement his mother treated him to a holiday abroad. The family hadn't much money and the boy had worked very hard to get where he was so she was very proud of him. Tragically he was killed whilst on holiday. He drowned in the sea, it was something to do with a tidal wave. Of course it wasn't the mother's fault, it was a freak accident and, as I tried to explain to the mother, his time had come. But the woman was inconsolable and racked with guilt. In her mind she had sent him to his death and I had a hard time convincing her otherwise. It was only when her son came through in spirit and told her again and again not to punish herself that she came to see that she was not directly responsible for his death.

Another mother I read for was terribly upset because she blamed herself for her sixteen-year-old daughter's death. She had insisted that the girl go on the contraceptive pill when she came of age and forced her to go and get it from the doctor. The girl had a boyfriend and naturally the mother was concerned that she might get pregnant. The mother hadn't wanted the girl to 'ruin her life' as she put it. Unfortunately the girl died later from a blood clot. The mother was certain that this had resulted from the Pill and so blamed herself entirely for her daughter's death.

I read for this woman because she was in so much pain and was so tortured. The message she had left for me on the answerphone had bothered me deeply and I was worried that she might do something drastic in a bid to make amends. I hadn't known how her daughter had died before the reading, but as soon as I got her daughter in spirit she made a point of telling me it wasn't her mother's fault. She kept telling me that she had a problem with her arteries and that she wanted her mother to see her doctors again and talk to them. I managed to give the mother some sense of comfort during the reading but I knew in my heart that she was still in a bad way and still felt like she had sent her daughter to her death. As she left I took her hand and told her to follow her daughter's advice. 'Go and see those doctors again,' I said as she left.

The woman did take her daughter's advice, and when she went to see the doctor the following week, it was explained to her that her daughter had a serious problem with her arteries, and whilst the Pill may have exacerbated this problem, it was so severe that her daughter didn't have much chance as it was. The mother told the doctor she blamed herself for telling her daughter to go on the Pill but the doctor explained that she couldn't have known and that if anything they were at fault for having prescribed it in the first place. Of course this information didn't bring the woman's daughter back to her, but it did stop her from tormenting herself with blame.

Too often parents torture themselves with guilt. Sometimes the guilt has nothing to do with the prevention of the death itself but manifests itself in other ways. With an older child, parents might feel guilty about the way they behaved to the child just before his or her death or even during their lifetime. Because we have a more complex relationship with our older children than we do with our very young, this type of guilt tends to be more prevalent in parents of older children. We might worry that we had been too hard on them, perhaps we had a row with our child before they died. We may feel guilty about not giving them enough time, or support; we may regret and feel guilty about the fact that we hadn't shown them enough love while they were still with us.

But once again we shouldn't punish ourselves about these things however guilty we feel. Spirits always forgive us for whatever happened at the time of their death. Arguments are always forgiven, fights forgotten and they know how much we love them.

Another reason why parents tend to feel so much guilt when they lose a child is because they always feel that it should have been them instead. All too often I have sat with grieving parents who feel guilty about the fact that their child is dead but they are still alive. They don't think it's right that they should be sitting in front of me, breathing, talking, living, whilst their child has been deprived of a future. Again this goes back to our instinctive belief in the natural order of life. It is natural for a parent, a grandparent or an adult to feel this way. Many parents I talk to say to me, 'Why couldn't it have been me?' or, 'If I had the choice I'd go in their place.' It's very normal to go through all these emotions but you have to keep remembering that your child went for a reason. Your guilt won't bring them back and wishing you were dead will not help either. For some reason, however painful it may seem, they were meant to go and you were meant to stay. Wishing you were dead as well may seem like the only thing that would make you happy, but it wont help anyone around you, such as your spouse or your other children. The child that has passed away would want you to try and be happy, especially for the rest of the family, and they would hate to think of you torturing yourself.

WHAT COULD HAVE BEEN

One of the hardest parts about losing a child is learning to overcome the regrets about what your child would have achieved had they lived on to adulthood. Parents who lose an older child torment themselves, quite understandably, with the notion of 'what could have been'. They mourn not just the loss of their child but the lost future that child would have had had they lived. 'What was the point of all those exams?' asks a mother who lost her child in a road accident three weeks after her son's GCSEs. 'In three weeks' time he would have started at university,' says another.

And so the examples and the questions go on. The boy who had just passed his driving test but was drowned on a school trip and never made it behind the wheel of a car on his own. The eighteenth birthday party cancelled, presents left unopened, because the girl died of meningitis days before. The gap year cut short by a fatal accident. The exam results that arrived after the funeral. And always I hear the same pitifully, painfully poignant lines: 'They had so much to live for,' and 'They had made so many plans.' The awful thing about losing a young person is that they always do have 'so many plans'. Young people are forever mapping out and planning their future, whether it's a trip to the pub, travelling round the world, getting engaged, going to a disco with a group of friends, starting at college or trying out for the school team.

This is all part of the nature of youth – planning what to do next, with the rest of your life. When that life is cut short and these unfulfilled plans fall into the shape of unused tickets, unopened birthday presents, unread postcards or exam results, the loss is all the more poignant. The tragedy becomes twofold. For the parent it is the loss of their child, for the child it is the loss of their future and their dreams. And we mourn them both.

We mourn what we consider our child to have been deprived of. That success at school, that degree course, their first job. The happy times they could and would have shared with their friends, the fishing trip they had planned, their first holiday without you. We mourn the sights and sounds they will never see, the countries they had planned to see but now won't. That first kiss or that first sexual encounter that we as adults still remember so vividly. Their first true love, their first heartbreak, their marriage. And we mourn the children they will never have too, and the happiness we know they would have derived from that.

As the years go by, these feelings, longings and regrets don't get easier to live with, they get worse. Ask any parent who has lost a child on the cusp of adulthood and they will tell you this – you cannot stop thinking about where that child would be now. And as you watch their friends and contemporaries move on, develop and become adults with lives, jobs and children, the thought of what could have been continues to haunt you.

In Chapter One I talked about the spirit world and what we are like in spirit. As I have said, if we die young when we reach the spirit world we carry on growing and developing until we reach the age of adulthood, which is twenty-one. The second thing to understand is that we are, in spirit, exactly how we were down here. Obviously, as I have explained, we are without pain and troubles, and there is no evil in the spirit world, but in essence we are exactly the same. If someone was by nature quiet and sensitive in this lifetime, they will be like that in spirit. If they were loud, cheeky or bubbly, they will be like that in spirit. When we die it is only our physical body that ceases to exist. The blueprint for who we are as people, our characteristics and personalities, are held within our soul and that part of us lives on.

I think many people who come for readings with me are taken aback by this. They are always surprised about how I am able to capture the personality of their child, their use of language, their expressions and so forth. What I try to explain to them is that I am not 'capturing' anything, this is what I am actually hearing. So if your child spoke in a particular way down here, maybe using slang or special words or expressions, then all this will come to me in the reading.

If we are the same in spirit as we were down here, when it

comes to our personalities then what we like, what we do, how we behave will be the same too. A young person who was good with children in this life, for example, will be good with spirit children in the next life. They will be the ones who care for the children in the spirit world. A young person who was gifted with numbers in this life will have that same gift in the next life. Those who wanted to help people by being a doctor or a nurse or a carer here on earth will fulfil that potential in the spirit world. Of course there is no illness in spirit so instead they help us down here. They are the ones who watch over us, make sure we go to the doctor in time, sound the alert in time, get you help when no one is around and so on. How do I know this, you may ask? I know this through the thousands of readings I have been involved with. Time and time again I will say to a parent, 'Your child is caring for children now,' or, 'They are showing me a garden full of plants,' and that parent will look at me in total disbelief and say, 'how did you know she wanted to be a nursery worker?' or, 'He had trained to be a gardener.'

When I read for a parent who has lost a teenager or older child, the readings always make them smile because these children simply don't change when they pass over. They are just the same as they were when they were with us down here. During a reading they can be quite cheeky and funny, they like to tease their parents and have a go at their younger brothers or sisters. All spirits visit us during the day and, as I say, they like to tell you what is going on at home to prove to you that it is them. Often they like to play practical jokes on their families. I once read for a father who lost his son in an accident. The father and son loved to wind each other up and play tricks on each other.

When the boy passed over, the father began to think that he was going mad because odd things kept going on around the house. He'd go to put some classical music on in the evening when the couple had guests round and instead one of his son's CDs would start blaring out the most unsuitable music, the type of record that comes with a parental advisory warning on the cover because the lyrics are so rude. Another time he went to a meeting and opened his briefcase to find that his papers had been replaced with pieces of fruit. The man didn't understand any of this and thought that either he or his wife had gone mad. But when they came to me for a reading these were the first things that the son mentioned to me and he kept roaring with laughter!

What I love about reading for parents who have lost a teenager is that it's just like being a fly on the wall at a typical family home. You will always get the slight squabbles about possessions and that kind of thing. The older child will be very aware of what's happened to his or her things, whether one of their younger brothers or sisters has taken something from their room, or borrowed a record or something. But it is all meant in good humour, and what I always say to parents is that it's nice because it means that they are still very much around you and taking part in family life.

On this note, it is very important when you lose a child not to bury their whole life all at once. Don't rush into getting rid of their clothes and possessions too soon. Just because we bury our children doesn't mean that we have to get rid of all of their life at the same time. Once a funeral has taken place it is good to be able to take some time out and have some space to think. When people are very upset they can get very determined about things and rash decisions can be made, ones we later regret. Whilst I don't think it's a good idea to create a mausoleum for your child and leave their bedroom untouched for years to come, I do think you should allow yourself some time and let things settle. The reason I say this hasn't got anything to do with the spirit or how they feel – it's really to do with you. You may feel after a time that there are certain things that your child had that you may want to keep. When you are more settled about what has happened you may want to give your child's clothes, for example, to one of their friends. Or it may be that there are some records in their collection that you and your family would like to keep as a reminder of them.

Spirits visit us the whole time, and the spirits of children who have passed away come to us quite often because they like to be with their families, but it is important to remember that spirits come to people, they don't come to rooms or houses. I say this because a lot of people get worried about moving house or dismantling rooms. You must not worry about this. Wherever you are in the world your child will come to you, and when they do come it will be with an enormous amount of love.

Paul's and Shelagh's story

Paul and Shelagh, two wonderful people from South Africa, lost their teenager daughter Kathleen in 1998 in the most tragic of circumstances and have had a terrible time, not only coping with the loss of their beloved daughter but also coming to terms with the horrific and traumatic way in which she lost her life, and the mystery that surrounded her death at the time. Their story is worth sharing because when they lost Kathleen, Paul and Shelagh had to go through a whole spectrum of emotions before they were able at last to accept their daughter's death. I have read for them now on a couple of occasions and each time I do, Kathleen, who is a bright and funny girl, always comes through with so much love and warmth for her family. Kathleen's father Paul starts the story.

Paul:

On the morning of Saturday 14 February 1998 our daughter Kathleen arrived home having spent the night with two of her closest friends, Kerry and Tara. She was in her usual bubbly mood, high-spirited and full of her zany humour. We had promised to tell her that day whether we would allow her to go on a yachting camp the following weekend. She bounced into our bedroom in an expectant mood, with an impish grin and pleading eyes but pretending to be serious. We gave our permission for her to attend the camp with our usual warnings about late-night parties and strange boys – the standard lecture parents have to issue their teenage daughters – and threatened all forms of terrible punishment if she did not behave. Mission accomplished, Kathleen excitedly telephoned her sailing friend Kelly to confirm the arrangements for the weekend.

After breakfast Kathleen set about her studies and we left her at home while we went shopping for groceries. We arrived home at midday and found her still hard at work for her May exams. Shelagh and I were not feeling too well so we both lay down for a while. Shelagh went to the spare room; I lay down in our bedroom. Kathleen asked Shelagh why she liked to rest in the spare room, and

Shelagh replied that it was because the room was bright, airy and peaceful.

Our plans for the afternoon were to drive to Vereeniging to visit two of Shelagh's school friends, Dave and Elaine. Dave had been the photographer at our son Steven's wedding in January and the purpose of the trip was to collect the wedding album. Vereeniging was about an hour's drive, so the trip was expected to take up most of the afternoon. Kathleen asked if she could stay at home to study rather than endure the long trip and afternoon tea with us 'old folks'.

Kathleen prepared lunch for the three of us and before we left she decided that she would visit another of her school friends, Justine. But Shelagh and I were not happy with the idea of her wandering around while we were away so we told her that she should remain at home. Not happy with this response, Kathleen initially argued the point and then finally gave up and accepted our decision. Shelagh and I left home at around 2 p.m. and then did something that was a complete departure from our normal custom. We called out to Kathleen from the front door. Normally we would have gone to kiss her goodbye. In another departure from habit, even though I had remembered to take the cellphone, we did not call Kathleen to make sure she was OK. I was restless during our visit to Elaine's. After about an hour there I felt an unexplained need to leave but we stayed on and in fact ended up leaving an hour later than we had originally planned. And even though this would mean we would be late coming back we did not call Kathleen to tell her.

At around 5.30 p.m. we stopped at a local supermarket to buy a few items for supper. I remember standing at the sweet counter for what seemed like an eternity trying to choose chocolate for Kathleen. We arrived home at 6 p.m. It was dusk. When we unlocked the front *door we were both struck by the fact that no lights were on even though it was getting dark, and there was a strange silence. Shelagh called out to Kathleen but there was no reply, only silence.*

As I walked past the spare room I noticed that the holster of my revolver was lying on the floor just inside the doorway. I felt very uneasy and immediately rushed to our bedroom. The door of the gun safe in the cupboard was wide open, the keys still in the lock. The gun was missing.

I called to Shelagh, saying that there was something very wrong, and I started running from room to room. My mind was full of dread. I had a horrible feeling that something terrible had happened.

I found Kathleen lying on the bed in the spare room. She looked peaceful with an almost surprised look on her face. In her right hand, lying limply on the pillow in the middle of a large bloodstain, was my revolver. Behind me Shelagh heard me cry out. She hadn't seen Kathleen yet but called out, 'Is she dead?' I touched her cheek without really knowing what to do and when I felt how cold she was I picked up her left hand to find it completely limp. Shelagh rushed to telephone for help from friends and neighbours. I stood over Kathleen's body, paralysed with shock and pain, wishing that I could wake up from this horrible nightmare.

The next few hours were a blur. Friends, family, our doctor, the priest, paramedics and police flooded into the house. Our neighbours were the first to arrive quickly followed by Anton, a psychologist and ex-policeman who thankfully was able to take charge of the situation. When the police had difficulty in negotiating Kathleen's long body onto the stretcher, Anton simply took her in his arms and carried her out.

In the days that followed we tried to piece together Kathleen's last moments. We tried to fathom how and why this had happened to our daughter. On the computer Kathleen had prepared Biology and Geography notes, her school books lay open on the desk. She had made a number of telephone calls to her friends, especially to Tara who was coming over to spend the night. Kathleen had been excited about their plans for the evening. She called her boyfriend who was also studying for his exams. All these conversations were quite normal. None of her friends noticed anything in her voice to suggest that there was something wrong. According to them Kathleen was her normal happy self planning things for the next few days, right up to the time of her death. There was no letter, just a couple of rough copies of letters to her friends, chatting about things in general.

We just could not understand it. We couldn't make sense of anything. Why had Kathleen taken the gun out? What was she doing with it? What happened? These were the questions that kept running through our heads, questions which will continue to torment us for the rest of our lives. Kathleen, our mature, serene bundle of joy, had gone. How were we going to live without her wonderful presence?

Six weeks after Kathleen's death Shelagh and I reached the point where the mystery surrounding her death became unbearable. We did not accept that Kathleen had committed suicide. Some might say we were in denial – it's hard for any parent to come to terms with that – but we just knew she hadn't taken her life. And what's more, the police agreed. Her death was not typical of any suicide that the police officers on the case had seen. Even Anton, the psychologist who had been coaching Kathleen on how to overcome exam stress, was shocked.

There were so many questions that we needed answers for and

we weren't getting them – until Shelagh contacted a psychic. She takes up the story . . .

Shelagh:

After that dreadful night our lives changed drastically. We were heartbroken, devastated. I didn't want to go on living. Paul withdrew into himself, became quieter than usual. Our son Steven was heartbroken and angry. His wife Bianca was still mourning the loss of her twenty-four-year-old aunt who had been killed in a recent riding accident. The whole family was traumatized.

Only three weeks before, Steven and Bianca had been married in the same church where we were now attending Kathleen's requiem mass. A church where we had all felt so much joy only a month before was now filled with so much sorrow. We were in the same pews. I was in the same dress, but this time it was to say our goodbyes to Kathleen.

And all the time the same questions were going through my head. Why did she have our revolver, why did she take it from the safe, what went wrong in those few hours?

Prior to her death I had always shown an interest in communicating with people on the other side, but I had never pursued it. I knew what I wanted to know, what I had to do, but where to start? I visited a psychic in Johannesburg and she confirmed (partially) what I had suspected – that Kathleen did not intentionally kill herself, that someone else was somehow involved. After that I needed to know more. Listening to our local radio station one day I heard the last few minutes of an interview with Rita Rogers. I took the station phone number and promptly phoned them. Rita had done a reading for a family in South Africa and the mother who was in the studio was called Pat Mulligan. Her son had been killed in 1993 when he was knocked off his bicycle by a car just before his seventeenth birthday. The family had flown to the UK to see Rita. The radio station was only able to give me Rita's postal address. The urgency in me now was growing to fever pitch. I had to contact her, I had to find Pat Mulligan, but once again . . . where to start?

Later on that week, Steven was reading a newsletter to me as I suffer from diabetic retinopathy and am almost blind. It was from the Compassionate Friends, an organization which brings together families who have suffered the loss of a child. He was finding it difficult as he was trying to deal with his grief in his own way but he carried on for me. He was reading the Death Anniversary column and suddenly came out with 'Ryan Mulligan . . .' I could not believe what I was hearing. 'Ryan Mulligan . . . son of Colin and Pat Mulligan.' And as if it was meant to be, there in print was Pat's phone number, and what's more, the Mulligans and their daughters Bronwyn and Kaylin lived in a neighbouring town. I just couldn't believe it. This wasn't just luck or a coincidence – someone was leading me to Rita. I phoned Pat immediately and she gave me Rita's phone number. I dialled it straight away but couldn't get through, so I rang and rang and kept trying until I eventually got through. It was as though someone was telling me to keep trying, not to give up. Eventually I reached Rita's daughter Kerry, and she told me I could have a reading in July of 2000. I was shattered. How was I going to survive for over a year? I told Kerry how desperate I was and that I was suspicious about Kath's death. She went through the diary again and told me that she could fix an evening reading for the family for two and a half weeks' time. I wept with joy. Kath was calling me. I knew it for sure.

The evening of the most important telephone call I have ever made in my life arrived. I had organized a speakerphone and Paul, Steven and Bianca gathered in the lounge with me. I put a tape recorder by the telephone, we were all nervous but we were ready. Very soon I would be in contact with Kathleen again. I had no doubts about it. Rita came on the telephone. She spoke for a while and explained how the readings were conducted, and then it was time. The first message: Mum, it was an accident.

A message came through from Kathleen's grandfather who asked about her grandmother's health and her knee in particular. (A year later Kathleen's grandmother's knee became so bad with arthritis that she became confined to a wheelchair.) Rita told us that Kathleen had been a bridesmaid at Steven's wedding. She spelled out the name BIANCA. Kathleen wanted to know about her new shoes. We had spent many fruitless hours searching for shoes for Kathleen to wear for Steven's wedding. She was also asking if her watch was there. I had ordered a new watch as a surprise for Kathleen's eighteenth birthday, something she never knew.

Rita asked if Kathleen took tablets or had injections because she was getting a message about this. Later she asked whether someone had poor eyesight. I explained about my diabetes, that I was on a lot of medication, and that I was almost blind from diabetes.

The names of Kathleen's friends, Kelly, Kerry, Tara and Jean, were mentioned. Rita then asked if our daughter's name began with the initial 'J'. Something stirred in me. I looked at Paul and then said no. Rita kept getting the 'J' long into the reading. When I asked Rita to ask by what name we called our daughter, her reply was truly amazing. She immediately said 'K' and then spelt out Kath's name, but Rita couldn't understand why Kath kept telling her 'J'. We could explain it, but we didn't tell Rita at that stage. Kathleen was adopted at the age of two weeks and the name her birth mother had registered her as was Jennifer.

Kathleen knew about her adoption – we had always been open with her. We had told her that when she was eighteen she could add the name Jennifer to her own name if she wanted. We felt that as it was from her birth mother she was entitled to it. She liked the idea a lot. Only Kath, Steven, Paul, Bianca and I knew about her registered name. We had chosen the names Kathleen Lauren for her.

Rita then went on to describe our home, referring to it as a bungalow-style house with a very long passage, and she told us about the carved wooden name plaques on Steven and Kathleen's bedroom doors.

Rita then moved on to the night that Kathleen died. She spoke about someone trying to force the front door and threatening Kathleen at the window where she was busy with her school work. That was correct. The computer was switched on and her biology book was open next to it. She was busy with a project and this was still on the screen. The desk was near the window. She also spoke about a white car in the driveway – she was referring to Paul's white Opel Astra, a car we had been planning to give Kathleen at the end of her school year.

At this point Rita started telling us about a CD of Kathleen's that Steven had borrowed not realizing that it actually belonged to Kath. It was Celine Dion's 'My Heart Will Go On', the theme song from the film Titanic. *It was Kath's favourite song and her friend was bringing this CD round on the day that she died. We had been given it after she died to play at the funeral service. We still think of it as Kath's CD and Steven was not aware of it until this message* now came from Kathleen. When I told Rita that we were all around the phone, she asked if Bianca was pregnant. Bianca wasn't but her younger sister was, and Rita's comment, 'Well, she is going to have a little girl,' proved to be correct.

Through Rita I think Kath knew that I needed more confirmation that it was really her we were talking to. Suddenly Rita said, 'Kathleen I don't know what you're on about – she keeps telling me "She's got my top on".' I was quite puzzled, but Bianca tapped me on the shoulder and told me she was wearing a knitted polo top that Kathleen had outgrown and handed on to Bianca. That was the proof I needed. It was a detail that Rita could not have known or guessed. It meant that we really were talking to Kathleen and that she was around us.

This knowledge that our daughter was with us was over-whelming. The tears started to flow. I wanted to reach out and hug Kathleen and ask her all sorts of questions. You cannot imagine the feelings that we experienced – joy, sorrow, heartache, longing, dis-belief – all at once.

The message that came through again and again was that Kathleen wanted everyone to know that her death had been an accident and that she had not committed suicide or been murdered. This was very important to Kathleen and of course to us. The time came to say goodbye, but I knew in my heart that I would talk to Rita again, and something or perhaps even someone was telling me inside that it wouldn't be on the telephone, but in person in the UK.

A trip to England to see Rita might have just remained a dream, but in 1999 Paul won an award at work which consisted of a cruise from Vancouver to the ports of Alaska, then back to South Africa via England. We had some time in England so I made an appointment to see Rita at her home in Derbyshire. Two days before we left for Vancouver I received a telephone call from a woman I had never met before, called Janine Gogos. She explained that her son had been hijacked and killed in October 1998. She asked whether I might be able to take a photograph of him to Rita and see if she was able to do a reading for her and her family. Naturally, I agreed. A chain was beginning to build up. I had met Rita through Pat, now Janine was coming to me. Three strangers linked by tragedy.

I asked Janine and her husband Con to come over straight away. The picture she wanted me to show Rita was of her son at his twenty-first birthday party in May 1998. I asked if they would like to see a picture of Kathleen. I led them to Kathleen's bedroom where I kept the photographs and also a candle burning. I explained to them that the lit candle brought me a certain amount of peace and Janine confessed that she kept candles burning for her son. While we were standing there in the room Con suddenly shivered and said that he could feel that the children were there together at that moment. It was almost as though they were orchestrating the whole visit, and I was suddenly overwhelmed by the presence of Kathleen.

Following our cruise, the day came when we left London by car to travel north to meet Rita. Once at the house Rita discussed things in general to relax us before starting the reading. Then she began. The very first thing she said to us was that Kathleen's death had not been intentional. It was not suicide, it was an accident. Once again she kept getting the initial 'J' from Kathleen and said that her name was something like Jenny. It was then that we told Rita about Kathleen's adoption and her birth name.

Rita then began to talk about the accident and went into a surprising amount of detail. She said a man of colour, approximately *thirty-five years of age, who sold vegetables or something like that, had startled and frightened Kathleen at the study window where she was sitting at the desk doing her school work. He started to threaten Kath, and then tried to force the front door open. Thank God it was locked!*

Rita told us that Kath went straight to our room, found the keys of the gun safe and in a desperate bid to protect herself took the revolver. She did not appear to think of calling for help but typically decided to look after herself. Kath was a child who was never afraid of anything. She knew no fear. In many ways Kath was mature for her seventeen and a half years. In other ways she was just a teenager trying to find herself.

After what must have been a long and stressful time, Rita told us that the intruder left the premises. Kathleen was telling her that she went to the spare bedroom, the bright peaceful room I had taken a rest in earlier that day. She was saying that she had been emotionally drained and, feeling the strain and the stress of this traumatic ordeal, she lay down on the bed, the loaded revolver in her hand. Exhausted by what had happened Kath fell asleep. She jolted awake, and in doing so Kath inadvertently pulled the trigger. The bullet entered her head and she died instantly.

At last we had the answers. It was as we had all thought: it was a terrible accident.

The reason I believe this is because Rita gave us details that she simply couldn't have made up, not only about the accident itself but about other things too. During the course of this second reading Rita told me that Kath was saying that she was worried about my eyesight. My diabetic retinopathy was now advanced and my sight had greatly deteriorated recently. She was pleading with Rita to tell me to go to an ophthalmologist, soon. I took her advice and the result was that I had a vitrectomy to both my eyes. This was a new procedure that removed the blood that haemorrhaged from the vessels in the back of my eyes and gave me clear, uninterrupted vision in the left eye. I now wear glasses, and with a pair of highly magnified reading glasses I am able to read some types of print, and this has been thanks to Kathleen and Rita.

During the reading Rita also referred to a 'Sally or Sophie' who she described as being like a second mother to Kathleen. She said that she loved this person as much as she loved us all. We knew who she was talking about. Sophie had worked in our home for the last twenty-five and a half years. Naturally Kathleen had spent a great deal of time with Sophie, practising her Zulu to their great mutual amusement and, yes, she was like a second mother to her.

Rita said that Kathleen was also very worried about my brother-in-law. She kept repeating that he was not well at all. She mentioned him by name and once again she was correct. When I returned to South Africa I phoned my sister and she said that her husband was recovering from hepatitis. Much later on he developed a liver abscess and was extremely ill. He had previously suffered from blackouts and these increased in severity to the point where he blacked out whilst driving and as a result crashed the car. He was then diagnosed with epilepsy and thanks to the medication prescribed to him is now in better health.

Rita also told us that there 'was another Paul in Kathleen's life'. She said that they were very good friends and were like soulmates. But we couldn't remember another Paul. After the reading Rita performed a transfiguration in which Paul and I saw Kathleen's straight nose and her gentle smile playing around her mouth and lips. *She was misty in form but it was definitely her. When I handed Rita Janine and Con's photograph of their son, she studied it quietly for a while and then declared without hesitation that he had been hijacked, that he had been shot by three men and that his vehicle had been stolen. She said that he had been shot three times. Everything she said collaborated with what we had been told about his death. Rita then turned the photograph over and exclaimed that this was the 'other Paul' in Kathleen's life. Paul and I looked at each other in amazement for until this moment we had forgotten that the Gogos' son was indeed called Paul! I believe now that Kathleen, Ryan Mulligan and Paul Gogos had met in spirit and had not only become friends but had each led us to Rita. (We booked a telephone reading for Janine and Con after this and once again their reading with Rita was incredibly accurate.)*

It is, I suppose, heart-warming to know that our children are out there and still with us and are happy. Our children had brought their parents together and that has helped Paul and me a lot. With each other's help we move forward and are learning to live again. It is extremely difficult, but knowing they are around us, thanks to these readings, has been incredibly encouraging.

5. Losing a Sibling

The relationship we have with our brothers and sisters is unique. There is a bond there which goes beyond anything we have in other kinds of relationships. It is a powerful and intense dynamic which begins at an early age, and with twins it is one that starts in the womb. The death of a sibling at any age can have a profound effect on us. Whether you are six or sixty when you lose your brother or sister, the pain you feel is always very intense.

The reason why you have such strong relationships with your brothers and sisters is that you share so much history and heritage with them. You have, after all, spent your childhood together and all the ups and downs that went with it. You have grown up together, from tiny children into adolescence. You have watched each other become adults, and if you are lucky you will have grown old together too.

Unlike the relationship you have with your friends, partners or soulmates you and your sibling have spent most of your life together. You have shared the same toys, clothes, house, the same parents and relations. You may have slept in the same room together when you were children. You may have gone to the same school. You have shared much of your life with your brother or sister, maybe even more time than you have with your own husband or wife. It is this shared experience which gives siblings their special bond. The common ground you have means that you don't have to 'forge' a relationship with your sibling because it already exists, unlike other relationships you may form throughout your life. You don't have to go through pleasantries, find out about what they are like, judge whether you will like them or not. With your sibling the relationship you have is already in place.

The strong bond we have with our brothers and sisters gets more intense as we get older. Even if we lose touch with our sibling that bond doesn't disappear. Even if you have drifted apart over the years, the history you share doesn't evaporate. What were once shared experiences now become shared memories.

Whether you got on with your sibling or not (and let's face it, we have all had moments when we have wanted to pull each other's hair out!), the loss of a brother or sister can hit us very hard. Perhaps harder than we might have imagined, because when our sibling dies we lose part of our life as well. We bury a whole part of our life when we lay them to rest.

The relationship between brothers and sisters is very complex. It involves so many more emotions than simply love. Our sibling, if we are lucky, may be our best friend, they might be our protector, or the one whom we feel protective towards. For much of our early life they are our closest companion, our ally against the outside world. If they are older than we are, they may be our mentor, the one we look up to, the one we are forever trying to impress, the one we idolize. If they are younger than we are, we may feel a deep affection for them and have almost parental feelings for them.

But sibling relationships also have their ups and downs. Within the dynamic of family life siblings fight for attention, for their voice to be heard above others. They constantly battle to be higher up in the emotional pecking order. They squabble, they fight, they resent each other. Even the closest of siblings can have their ups and downs. And on top of this there is sibling rivalry. Your sibling is, after all, the person you are most often compared with – by your parents, family and friends and even by yourself – whether it is over when each of you walked, the length of your mother's labour, at what age you learnt to read. So your sibling is not just a relation, but a benchmark.

Within families each sibling fulfils a certain role. When I was growing up there was a very clear-cut pecking order in our family. As one of the oldest I was expected to take care of the younger children and set an example for them. This role was further exacerbated by the fact that I was a girl. Both my mother and father expected me to keep an eye out for the younger boys and to take care of them when their hands were full. I didn't mind this role at all as I adored all my younger brothers and I was happy to help out. But what's funny about that role is that it has never really changed. I still make sure the younger children are all OK and with my mother now gone I have adopted an almost matriarchal role in our family. When I think about my youngest brother Stephen I still think of him as the baby of our family, even though he is a grown man with a family and a career.

So the roles that we adopt as children within the family unit don't really change as we grow older, and can have an effect on the way we deal with the loss of a brother or sister. For example, the loss of the elder sibling might feel to the younger ones like the loss of a parent. Alternatively the loss of the youngest sibling might feel like the loss of a child to the others (especially if the age gap has been quite large). And the loss of any middle children in a large family will affect siblings in completely different ways. In my experience I find that the loss of a younger sibling can be as upsetting for the older siblings as it can for the parents, because the death of younger members of the family upsets the natural order of things. We are instinctively programmed to believe that we will go before younger siblings, so if they pass away before us we can be quite disturbed by it.

The relationship we have with our brothers and sisters is really quite spiritual. An element of this comes from the fact that we are related – if we are natural brothers and sisters then we have shared the same womb, which I do feel can strengthen the link we have – but even if we aren't full brothers and sisters, even if we have been adopted, or are *half-* or *step* brothers and sisters, that bond is still very strong because we were destined to be part of the same family unit and to grow up together. The relationship between brothers and sisters is spiritual in another way too. Because we grow up together we know a great deal about one another. Right from the beginning we seem to be able to judge our siblings' moods, to know what they are thinking, to understand how they are feeling without actually having to articulate this in normal conversation.

In my other books I have talked at length about the special bond that exists between twins and how twins have a very psychic relationship with each other, but this kind of link doesn't exclusively belong to twins – other siblings have it too. Although it might not be quite as strong, there does seem to be a degree of telepathy between siblings. This may come from the fact that we have spent so much time together or because even before we were able to talk we were able to 'read' our brothers and sisters. Time and time again people tell me of their uncanny ability to know what their brothers and sisters are thinking or doing. Sisters who are close will say that they are able to know when one of them is about to call, they might instinctively know when one of them is pregnant even though there are as yet no signs. They might know when one is hiding something from the other, or lying about something. Brothers may be able to read how the other is feeling even though no words are spoken, and so it goes on. We talk of being able to know 'when something isn't right' or that 'something was on their mind'. We feel when they are unhappy even though they are hiding it from us, we sense they are in trouble even though we haven't heard from them in months. Between siblings, sometimes a silence can say much more than words can.

So if this is what it is like when your sibling is alive, you can imagine what it is like when I read for siblings. These readings are always very strong and clear and the brother or sister will be very quick to make contact with me. What I love about these readings is that they are full of the most amazing details. As with any other reading, the spirit will want to prove to you that you are indeed talking to them, so they will make the usual points of reference. They will tell me who they are with in spirit even if these people do not come through themselves. They might tell me what you have been doing lately to prove that they have visited you. But they also talk a lot about the past. There will be so many shared jokes, references to the names of cuddly toys or pets you had, names of school friends you shared and so on. Out the details come, one after the other, and to be quite honest I have no idea what they are about because it all seems like madness to me, but I know as I watch a smile form across someone's face that it means a great deal to them. I have sat here in my reading room with people who are terribly upset and full of tears when their reading starts, only to have them beaming from ear to ear five minutes later. I once read for a woman who had lost her older brother. She seemed so unmoved by the reading to start with that she just sat there and didn't show any emotion whatsoever. I was repeating to her what her brother was saying to me, which meant nothing to me at the time, when suddenly she burst into floods of tears. 'Are you OK? Would you like me to stop?' I asked tentatively, fearing it was all too much for her. 'No, she said, please go on!' It turned out that her tears weren't those of sadness. Her brother was teasing her about something that had happened when they were teenagers and she was laughing so much she had started to cry!

LEARNING TO LIVE WITHOUT YOUR SIBLING

People often don't realize how traumatic losing a sibling is. They tend to assume that in one way or another we will be able to pick ourselves up and just get on with life. They forget how close the relationship between siblings can be. When a young child dies in an accident we think first about how his parents must be feeling and our hearts go out to them. Rarely do we stop and think how his twelve-year-old brother is feeling, or imagine how he is confronting his loss. Yes, the parents have lost their child, which is terrible, but the brother has also lost someone too. A brother he shared his life with, a playmate and a friend. Similarly, when a woman dies of cancer we immediately think of her children and her husband. How will that family cope now that she has gone, we ask ourselves, so we ring to see if they are OK, we send them flowers, we write them letters. But what about her brother and sister, how are they feeling now? The older brother who adored his little sister, who spent his childhood teasing her, bullying her, telling on her, yet deep down always loved her so much. And her older sister, the one she called every night and first thing every morning. Who will call her now, who will she confide in, and who will she go to the shops with on a Saturday morning?

I am not saying that siblings feel the loss of their brother or sister *more* than their parent – of course they don't – but that they feel the pain and the loss *just as much*.

When we have shared so much of our lives with one person it can be very hard to let go. You have known your sibling since childhood, so when you suddenly lose your brother or sister it can be difficult to adapt. Suddenly there is no one to share those family problems with or those jokes that you have had since you were little. There is no one to call when you are worried about your mother, no one to borrow something from. Suddenly there is this great big void in your life: one that cannot be filled by anyone else. Learning to live without your sibling can be a very difficult thing to do.

In the summer of 2000 I did a reading for a journalist called Justine Picardie. Married with two young children, Justine had come to me because she wanted to communicate with her sister, Ruth. Ruth had died from breast cancer when she was only thirty-three, leaving behind a husband and their twins. Before she died Ruth had written about her illness in a column in the *Observer* magazine, called 'Before I Say Goodbye'. I never read the column, but apparently it had a great following and people were very moved by Ruth's story.

When Ruth eventually lost her battle and died, Justine was obviously very upset and missed her sister a great deal. She went to bereavement counselling, psychotherapy, took antidepressants and tried alternative medicine, but none of this seemed to help her. She wanted desperately to be able to communicate with her sister and so she started to visit mediums and psychics in an attempt to find someone who could communicate with Ruth. Justine wrote about this journey to find Ruth in her book *If the Spirit Moves You*. There she talks about her reading with me:

Nothing could have prepared me for the tidal wave of grief that came crashing down when my sister Ruth died of breast cancer at the age of 33. I had known other deaths – terrible, tragic, early deaths, like hers – yet I was to learn that every bereavement is different; and the loss of Ruth left me feeling almost unable to go on living. After she died, I struggled through my day-to-day existence: caring for my children, going to work, trying to understand what seemed like the impossible task of life without my sister.

As the months passed, I began to accept that she was dead – but what I couldn't accept was her silence. We had always talked so much, Ruth and me, me and Ruth, about everything and nothing. When we knew that her cancer was terminal, we promised each other that we would still speak after she died – because silence was unthinkable. Yet two years after her death, still the silence was unbroken.

It was then that I started investigating mediums and spiritualists (a journey which I describe in my book If the Spirit Moves You*), and finally came across Rita Rogers, via a friend who had been much helped by her. By this point, I was becoming sceptical about the various people who had promised that they could hear the voice of my sister: however much I wanted to believe them, nothing quite rang true. But when I finally spoke to Rita on the phone on a blue-skied June morning, something magical seemed to happen. Quietly, gently, she began to name my friends and family who had died – and when she came to Ruth, my doubts began to melt away like ice in early sunshine. It was the little domestic details that felt so real: the name of Ruth's children's school (a name I had myself forgotten until then); a characteristic comment about their shoes (she was always adamant that they should be properly shod); and more, far more, private references to family matters that no one else could have guessed.*

At the end of my conversation with Rita, I felt as if she had brought Ruth back to me; or rather, she reminded me that Ruth had never left me; had always been there, waiting to be heard. It was – and is – the greatest gift: an indelible engraving upon our hearts of those we have loved, and still love, beyond death, beyond everything . . .

As Justine points out, it's the silence that is so painful. We can prepare ourselves for the death of a sibling and we can learn to accept death. But nothing really prepares us for the emptiness. In

Chapter Two I talked about how the grieving process can affect someone who has watched and nursed their loved one through illness, and how when they pass they are left with this terrible hole, this void. But this time has to be filled, the love they have for the person who has gone has to be channelled, though they mourn the loss of someone to talk to. Justine and Ruth were obviously very close – they had a special bond that was different from any other relationship they would have had with, let's say, their husbands or other friends. They had grown up together, been there for each other at the start of their careers, during each other's relationships and as young mothers. And their relationship was unique in another way: having watched Ruth grow up and become the woman she was, witnessed her marriage, seen her become a mother, Justine then had to watch her sister, who was on the cusp of so much, prematurely lose all that right in front of her eyes.

We know our siblings in ways other people don't. We see them with different eyes. We are much more aware of their vulnerabilities than other people are. We have a better understanding of their weak spots and their strengths. We know when they are putting on a brave face, when they are in pain and when they are really hurting.

Debbie's and Nicola's story

In the summer of 2002 I received a letter from a lady in Oxford. I had been going through my post one afternoon, sifting through the hundreds of letters I get daily asking for readings. As much as I would like to read for the majority of people that write to me, I can't, as it would be physically impossible. I already have a long waiting list and I find readings very draining. I am not prepared to squeeze in as many readings as possible in a day just for the sake of it. I am not doing this for the money, I am here to help people, so if I can't put a hundred per cent into a reading then I would rather not do it. I need time to be able to concentrate on each and every reading I do. If a reading takes three hours then so be it, but I am not prepared to cut corners.

The day this letter arrived I had no intention of reading for anyone. I had had a bad couple of months what with one thing and another, and I had been working overtime to fit in all my appointments. I had a much needed holiday booked and had planned to keep my diary free for at least a couple of weeks. And then, on top of all this, our family had been going through some very difficult times of our own. With one of my daughters ill, my whole focus was on her and getting her better. I didn't have time for others. For the first time in years, instead of helping other people with their problems I was trying to come to terms with my own. That said, I always try to keep up with my correspondence.

I have said that I didn't want to read that day but as soon as I picked up the two sheets of cream writing paper sent to me from Oxford I knew that I was about to break my pact with myself, for the moment I selected that letter to open a spirit came to me and would not let me alone. The letter was from a lady called Debbie and she was writing to me asking for help. She said that her cousin Jo had died only three weeks earlier and the whole family was naturally devastated. But she was not writing to me asking me for a reading for herself, she was asking whether I might be able to help Jo's sister Nicola. Nicola couldn't cope with the loss of her sister at all; in fact only the day before she had tried to commit suicide and was now in hospital.

She is broken, Rita, she is like a fragile little bird and I am so afraid for her welfare. She feels she cannot carry on without Jo and is just so heartbroken. I know very well that you are under pressure from so many people and I feel guilty writing to you, but I would be eternally grateful if you could find the time to talk to her. I would drive to the ends of the world to bring some peace to her and her parents. And I'm sure if she knew Jo was safe and no longer suffering, as her death was so distressing, it would help so much.

I put the letter down and stared out of the window. I knew this girl was in real trouble, if not danger. I knew that if I left it even a day she would perhaps take her own life. And with a compulsion that must have come from this Jo, I picked up the telephone and dialled the number and got hold of Debbie. She continues the story:

Debbie:
I had a phone call on 18 June 2002 at about 7.30 a.m. from my mum. It was a Tuesday morning. I'd been anxious the day before as my cousin Jo had been in hospital and was having a really rough time with her asthma. 'Deb, something terrible has happened . . . Joanne died last night,' she said in a very quiet and wavering voice.

119

I just couldn't believe what I'd heard. Time seemed to stand utterly still. The shock was so intense it made me feel physically sick. I didn't know what to say, there were no words.

Our entire family had been crushed that day, a horribly deep pain filled us all and there was nothing anyone could do to ease it. It didn't feel real somehow. Instead, it felt like a terrible dream that we would all wake up from and it wouldn't be true. I remember embracing uncle Bert, Jo's dad, that afternoon in my mum's garden with my sister Vicki and wanting so desperately to take away his sorrow, I'd never seen him cry, but we all, Mum included, cried with him.

I felt instantly afraid for my cousin Nicola who had been so close to Jo. As sisters they were inseparable, always together, and seemed like two halves of the same thing. Nicola was hurting so much. The first time I saw her was a few days before the funeral. She'd been out of the office since that terrible day and so had I – we work together and she had dropped in on the Monday to see everyone for a short while. She seemed so lost. Privately I kept thinking that I wished there was some way in which Nicola could say goodbye to her for Jo had died so tragically and unexpectedly. Mum told me about a lady who wrote a column in a popular women's magazine and that this lady gave readings for people who had lost loved ones – the lady in question was called Rita Rogers. I remembered seeing Rita on some sort of documentary on the TV one evening about a year ago and the feature was all about her gift – I had been transfixed. I had always had a very deep interest in the afterlife and spiritualism generally, particularly after loosing a close and young friend, John, to bowel cancer some five years previously.

The very painful day of Jo's funeral came and went – it was a beautiful service and a marvellous tribute to her, but at the same time very upsetting and it seemed that it shouldn't be happening. Nicola looked so empty and shattered, as did her parents. A few days afterwards I decided to find out more about Rita and ordered a couple of her books through our local book store. The books arrived within a couple of days and I read From One World to Another *overnight, I just couldn't put it down and I intended to pass it to Nicola, hoping that it wasn't too soon to do so.*

Nicola had been coming into the office and was trying hard to bury her head in work, but her grief was deep and getting harder by the day to bear. Saturday morning came and I received a phone call from my mum at about 8.30 a.m. 'Deb, something awful has happened – it's Nin (we call Nicola Nin, don't know why but we always have), she's not gone, but she's in hospital – she tried to commit suicide last night by cutting her wrists.' 'God, I hope Nin's OK, poor little thing.' I was gutted. Not again. I pondered for a moment and then told Mum I felt the time was right to write to Rita, and that I should do so without delay.

I chatted with my mum some more, put the phone down and started writing explaining just how I felt and how desperate we were for her help. I missed the post on Saturday morning, so couldn't send it till Monday. I asked Nin for permission to send the letter, and enclosed a wonderful picture of her and Jo together – I cried so much when I wrote that letter.

Nicola came out of hospital later on the Saturday and had a terrible wound to her left forearm, a deep cut that had needed nine stitches. She had been at the family ceremony the day before to bury Jo's ashes and the day's events had just been all too much for her to cope with. She had become very upset late in the evening and couldn't bear the thought of life any longer without Jo; thankfully a vigilant friend, Michael, was in the house and his interception and quick thinking ultimately saved her life. She was at that point truly broken. I think she had reached the lowest point she ever would.

The letter sent, I went to bed on Monday evening and before I went to sleep I talked to Jo, hoping that she could hear me wherever she was. I told her I had written to Rita and that when she received the letter the next day, Jo should try hard to communicate with her and ask her to call Nin.

I also talked to my friend John who had passed over five years previously and asked him to come through and let me know he was OK, should Rita ever call; I asked the same thing of my nan who I loved dearly and who was also named Rita.

I thought about Jo a lot on Tuesday. Nicola was in the office as she preferred to keep herself busy, but she was feeling very sore and very low. I knew it was too much to expect any results from my letter, but at about 9.05 p.m. that night my husband answered the phone. 'Deb, it's for you,' he said, 'it's Rita Rogers.' I couldn't believe it. I raced to the phone and picked it up. I said hello and listened to that wonderful voice. Rita told me she had been trying to contact Nicola; she said that since receiving the letter and reading it Jo had been with her – around her house and in her reading room. She said Jo was quite insistent that Rita should call Nicola. Rita told me that Jo had been coming through strongly throughout the day, she told me that Jo was OK; I can't tell you how relieved I was to hear that – I felt really choked.

Rita wanted to talk to Nicola soon. She said she had tried her mobile and her home number and she wasn't answering the phone. I told Rita she had gone out with friends for the evening but was *working in the office the next day and Rita said she would call back on the office number tomorrow. Before she put the phone down she said, 'Who's John?' I said I had an Uncle John but she said the person she was referring to was in spirit, that he had died young and that after being diagnosed with a condition had gone downhill very rapidly – my friend John had come through! 'He's coming through to let you know he's OK, he's happy and he sends his love, did he and Jo know each other in this life?' she asked. I told her that they had met and she confirmed that they certainly knew each other on the other side. 'Who's Nick?' asked Rita. 'Nicola?' I replied. 'No,' said Rita, 'he's giving me a Nick or Nicholas.' I confirmed that Nick was my husband and Rita told me that he was my soulmate and that John was very impressed with how Nick was doing with the business – Nick set up a successful business locally, but hadn't started it until after John's death.*

John told us he was really pleased for us and that all our hard work was paying off – he said things would get better and better. He also said that Nick and I had met at odd times and in different circumstances and were ultimately destined to meet. Rita then asked me who the letter 'E' corresponded to – I couldn't think. My mind was buzzing. But after I had put down the phone I remembered – it was Ellis, my son. We had named him after John, whose middle name was Ellis. John passed away when I was seven months pregnant and after a difficult labour and delivery when Nick was asked by the midwife if we had a name for our new baby boy he exclaimed 'Ellis!' I wasn't about to disagree since Nick had suffered an awful panic attack in hospital just prior to Ellis's delivery. John had introduced us and he must have wanted to show his approval.

My grandmother also came through, sending her love to all the family and saying that she had been there to collect Jo. Rita ended the conversation saying that she would call Nicola the next day for a reading – she felt she just had to. I was awe-struck. Rita didn't need to tell me any of the things she told me – she felt she just had to because these people were coming through to her as we spoke. Rita is a truly gifted medium, a wonderful lady who had no prompting from me at all. She simply relayed messages that were coming through from the three people I had thought so deeply about the day before.

Wednesday came and I jumped every time the phone rang at work. Mid-morning I answered the phone and heard that delightful voice again 'Is that Debbie? It's Rita Rogers here.' We spoke for a short while and Rita told me about her work and the projects she had under way. She's such a fantastically easy lady to speak with – I felt, like many others I'm sure, that I had known her all my life, and her words brought with them so much comfort. I put Rita on hold and ran upstairs to Nicola – I asked her to turn her radio off and ran to the bathroom to grab her some hankies. 'Rita's on line one for you,' I said. Nicola had been forewarned that she might be getting a call so as not to shock her, but she was very eager to take the call. The rest is her story . . .

Nicola:

I picked up the phone and said, 'Hello.' Rita introduced herself and told me all about what she does. She told me that she had connections with people who had passed on and she wanted to help. Rita didn't sound anything like what I had expected to hear – she sounded so down-to-earth and normal; I had imagined a really dramatic kind of person and she was just so easy to talk to. She reassured me, as best she could, before she started the reading.

Rita started by telling me about the little boy who had passed on and wanted her to call his mummy telling her that he wasn't cold any more. I understand this story features in one of her books. The little boy's mum had been to the chapel of rest and was upset at how cold he was – the little boy hadn't yet been buried – and he wanted to assure her he was OK. I was really taken aback.

Rita told me that Jo was a tomboy and went on to describe her perfectly. I was gobsmacked – how did she know these things? She then went on to say that Jo was happy and that she had made a lot of friends since passing over and that she was OK where she was. It was such a relief to hear that and I cried. Rita told me that a lady with the same name as her was there to collect Jo – that was my nan Rita; she had passed over more than twenty-five years previously at the age of fifty-one. Rita then mentioned a Deborah Ann, and that she sent her love to that person – that person is my cousin Debbie who initially wrote the letter to Rita. My nan Rita came through to send her love to the whole family and to say that she was there for Jo and they were spending time together. Rita (the medium) went on to say that Jo loved kids – I confirmed that – and that there was a special one in Jo's life, with a name beginning with the letter 'M'. Jo was due to become godmother to a baby she adored – Morgan. Jo also said to send her love to a woman who meant a lot to her called Margaret. I said, 'That's Maggie, who Jo shared a house with – Morgan's grandmother.' Rita also went on to say that Jo was looking after children now on the other side and that she was a good teacher.

Rita said Jo was saying something – she listened and then said she was saying, 'It's just like me not to have money!' I laughed, 'She never did have any bloody money!' I said, and Rita told me that there was no such thing on the other side. Jo was always complaining about being broke.

Rita then went on to say that Jo was telling her about a place surrounded by fields and horses. She said that she liked spending time there. Initially I thought that she must be talking about my aunt's garden – she has horses at the end of it – but then it struck me that the cemetery where we buried her ashes was surrounded by fields with horses in, and I had said to her on the day we buried her ashes, 'I hope this place is OK for you and that you like it here.' I feel now that she was answering that question for me. Rita told me that Jo was with a pet that we used to have beginning with the letter 'L' and that she was taking her for walks. We've only had one pet dog and she died some four or five years ago – her name was Lucy. Rita told me that I was sleeping at night with something that Jo used to wear. She told me that I was sleeping with a T-shirt of Jo's that I took to bed every night – which was true. Jo used to wear it in bed and it hadn't been washed so I could smell her on it. Nobody knew about that – only Jo could have if she had been there to see it. By this time I was speechless and on a real high, even though I was crying – the relief was so intense. I had expected Rita to tell me trivial stuff that anyone could have guessed, but she was giving me such firm facts.

Rita told me that Jo was telling her we were thinking of getting a dog – true again. Rita said she wanted us to call it Josie. Jo told Rita to tell Mum that she sent her love and that she had met up with my granddad Bill on the other side and that he was fine and spending time with her. Rita mentioned that I had two other half-sisters but no brothers, and that my mum was formerly married to a man called Eric – all true. Rita said I had just split up from a long-term relationship with a man beginning with the letter 'N'. This was true, but she said she was sending me my soulmate. She gave me details of this person which are personal to me.

Jo talked about Patricia Ann, my aunt, and said to send her love. Jo sent her love to Dad and told me to tell him to try and pick himself up because she was OK. I think she was worrying about him – she always did.

She said that Jo was well travelled and that she had travelled to Australia and wanted to travel to America. That was her next destination – apparently she still intends to go. We were due to go back to Australia in 2003 but Jo came through to say she still wanted me to go, even on my own, as she would be there with me. Jo then went on through Rita to say that I was destined to work with animals as we were both well into animals, and always had been since being very small.

Jo felt she had to tell me that her condition had been aggravated prior to going to hospital. She had a bad chest infection at the time and had passed on after a series of asthma attacks – she had not responded well to treatment at all. Jo told me she didn't know she was going to die, which was very hard for me to take in, and she was still very shell-shocked by all that happened. She told me, though, that she now knows she was not destined to live a long life.

Jo said she liked the fresh flowers that we keep for her in our living room – we always keep them and Jo's photos surround them. She also said to say thank you to Deborah Ann for the candle she keeps lit by her photo – she likes looking at it. She also mentioned small children with names beginning with the letters 'E' and 'N' – Debbie's two small children Ellis and Nina. She said she liked spending time with them.

Jo had a special friend she met through college night classes whose name was also Debbie and Jo sent her love and thanked her for the flowers that she left at the cemetery on the day her ashes were buried.

Jo said that she was glad Dad had decided to carry on the payments for her new car – she was so, so proud of it, it was a black Golf and her pride and joy. She also told me that I had bought a new car but didn't have it in my possession at that time – which was correct, as it was in the garage. Jo was glad because she wanted me to be safe while I was driving.

The reading finished with Jo telling me that I mustn't hurt myself by taking my own life because she wouldn't be able to be there to collect me. She could only be there for me when it was naturally my time. She made me promise not to hurt myself again and told me that I would live to be an old woman – that worried me a bit because I couldn't bear the thought of meeting her being old and her being young, but now I understand that I will be in my prime again when we next meet. She also said she'd let me know she's with me by touching the top of my head.

The whole experience of having this reading left me stunned but in a nice kind of way. I felt so comforted and, at the time, elated. One of my main worries was that after the manner in which Jo passed over she would still be suffering and unhappy, or that she had got lost – she was never any good at finding her way anywhere! It was a relief to know that she is OK and that she is happy and that ultimately she is with me. Times are still very difficult and I have to take every day as it comes – some are harder than others. I feel this experience has made things a little easier to bear. I know that the reading has brought a lot of comfort to other members of my family.

I know without a doubt I was talking to Jo – there was no way Rita could have known any of that stuff without Jo telling her. I hope very much to talk to Rita again some day soon.

6. *Losing a Parent*

I miss my mother terribly. When I am very down, scared or anxious about something I really wish that I could pick up the telephone and talk to her. Mum died when she was in her sixties and it was a terrible blow for me. That might seem strange to some people. I am, after all, a grown woman and have a family of my own. I shouldn't really need my mother still, you might say. Well, the fact is I do, and I will do till the day I die. The relationship between parent and child is a very special one. I really don't think it matters how old you are when it happens – losing a parent can be very distressing.

The bond between parent and child is very strong. We come after all from their own flesh and blood: there is part of them in us. Even if we are adopted then we are destined to be with our parents. Our parents are the ones who bring us into this world, and because of that we have an extraordinary dynamic with them. We owe them so much and yet can blame them for so much too. As their offspring we hold them accountable for how we turn out in the end. We may thank them for many things, but we may also hold things against them. The relationship between parent and child is unique. As parents they shower us with love and affection, they provide for us and protect us, they discipline us and they reward us. They make us who we are today.

Over the years the relationship between parent and child evolves from the uncomplicated love between parent and young child, through the challenges of adolescence to a more complex dynamic again as we get older. But throughout all this the fundamental relationship between parent and child never really changes that much: whatever age you are they are always your parents and you are always their child. To our parents we are always their children no matter how old we are. It's as simple as that.

I have said that we all miss our parents when they die no matter what age they are, but of course it is particularly tragic if you lose your parent when you are just a child. I am not a great one for reading for children. I wouldn't want to read for anyone unless they were fully aware of what I was doing. A reading could be terrifying for a child. But when I read for a person with young children who has been widowed, the parent who has died will always come through and tell me what is going on in their children's lives. In spirit they still act as a parent taking care of their children like a guardian angel and I find that they visit them a great deal because they hate to miss out on what they are doing.

When we are very young and we lose a parent it is much easier to adjust. Very small children accept their parent's absence much more easily than older children do. I know this from when my husband died. Little Kerry, who was only five and a half, didn't really understand what was happening or where her daddy went, and by the time I had met Mo she was ready to have another father figure in her life. But for the others it was much harder. They had known their father for longer and his death was very difficult to come to terms with. Adolescents can take a bereavement like this very badly. Because they are so highly strung at this stage of their lives they can be very oversensitive. Rather than crying or being sad or depressed, it is quite common for an older child to show their emotions in other ways such as getting angry or feeling betrayed. They might take it all out on the parent who has been left behind, which can be very upsetting. Remember that they are only behaving like this because they feel so hurt and raw, and the best thing you can do in this situation is be on standby to offer them as much love and support as you can.

Losing a parent creates the most terrible hole in one's life and it is one that can never be filled. That is what's so sad about losing your mother or father. The relationship you have had with them has been so exceptional that there will never be anyone in your life who will be able to fill their shoes. Think about it for a moment. Your parents have known you longer than anyone else in the world has. They have watched you grow from a tiny little thing into a person. They know everything about you. They have seen your triumphs and watched you fall. And what's more, because there is a little bit of them in you they understand you better than most. Our parents, having loved and nurtured us, have seen us at our most vulnerable. They were there to answer our cries as little babies, to put plasters on our knees when we had fallen, were on call to nurse that first broken heart. That is why we miss them so much when they go. We miss them when we are down and broken. We need them there for the bad times. And we also need them there for the good ones. It saddened me that Dennis wasn't able to give his girls away at their weddings or see his grandchildren. And I often find myself saying, 'Oh, I wish Mum were here to see this.'

It's when it comes to dealing with my girls that I miss my mum the most. She was always so great about giving me advice about what to do with them, whether it was something small, like being a bit naughty, or something more serious like being ill. Her death made me realize just how strong you have to be to be a parent. Sometimes it's exhausting trying to be strong the whole time, and what was great about having Mum around was that I could be a parent for the girls but as soon as they were out of earshot I could go running to Mum to be a child and lean on her!

When anyone in our family gets ill I always make an egg custard. Don't ask me why. I suppose I do it because Mum did. The funny thing is that even though I have been making this for years and years, I still can't remember how many eggs to put in it. Every time I made it in the past I would call Mum and ask her. She must have got so annoyed! But every time I make it now and I think I'd better call Mum for the recipe again, I have to remember that she has gone. And as soon as that happens I can hear her in my head sighing, 'Two eggs to half a pint of milk, Rita.'

As much as I adored Mum, I did sometimes jokingly wonder whether I was hers at all or whether she had just found me under a bush, for we looked nothing like each other. Mum had the figure of a model. She was absolutely tiny, about six stone, with a whippet-thin waist yet curves in all the right places. She had wonderful peroxide hair and always kept her nails varnished. She was like a little starlet, very particular about the way she looked. Even when times were really tight she'd be there in her immaculate cream pinny having bathed every day. She didn't ask for much – all she ever wanted was a house full of kids. That's all that mattered to her. 'Never moan about your kids and the finger marks they leave on the walls because all too soon they have grown up and gone,' she would say.

Mum loved a Guinness. 'The night I don't have my Guinness, Rita, is the night I'm going,' she used to say. And sure enough, the night before she died, Mum refused her drink. When I spoke to her that afternoon I sensed that something was wrong but she didn't say anything. She was not one for complaining. I knew Mum wasn't afraid to go because we had spoken about it from time to time. She was one of eight girls and I know that she longed to see her sisters in spirit again.

The next day I got a call from my brother Michael. 'Don't be alarmed, but Mum's in hospital,' he said. It was a very foggy day and I hate driving when it's like that so Michael had said not to come. 'She'll be fine, the doctors have said so,' he insisted. I was having a rest when he called me, but after that conversation I just couldn't relax. A couple of hours later I got up, got dressed and called to Mo. 'Right, we're off, we're going to the hospital right now.' Mo knows better than to disagree with me at times like this. Though the fog was as thick as pea soup outside he knew that he would have to get me there whatever it took. Once I have my mind set on something then that's it. I'm like a dog with a bone.

Kerry, Mandy and I got in the car with Mo at the wheel. I hate it when he drives fast, but that day I didn't care and told him to put his foot on it even though the poor man couldn't see a thing. One red light too many and I knew that we wouldn't make it there in time, and I was right. We got to the hospital and

I don't know what happened to me, it was like I had a tracking device inside me. I raced down corridors, barged through double doors and round wards as though I knew instinctively where to go even though I had never been there, and despite the fact that this, like most hospitals, was built like a maze.

I got to the ward just in time and found Mum behind a screen. 'Oh, she's fine, Mrs Rogers, really she is,' said a nurse, but I knew she wasn't. Round her bed were gathered all her boys, and on her bedside table were all our teddies that she had kept when we had left home. I took her hand, still with its immaculate red nail varnish, and she looked me in the eye and smiled and with that she passed away. It was as though she was waiting for me. She wouldn't have wanted her boys to have been on their own – she was waiting for me so that there would be a woman there for them. She was like that. Then a very odd thing happened. A nurse came up to me who had just started her shift. She wasn't the duty nurse and she hadn't talked to Mum, but she came over and looked at her and said, 'She'll be happy, now, she'll be with all her sisters.' I couldn't believe it. 'You've never been so right!' I replied.

Sharon's story

Sharon came to me through my daughter Mandy. They both have pet bulldogs and because of this had become friends. I hadn't met Sharon before and Mandy hadn't mentioned her to me, but when Mandy called me one day and asked me to read for her friend Sharon I agreed. Mandy didn't say much to me.

She told me her name, mentioned something about the dogs but said that she was quite upset about something and needed to talk to me. I didn't ask her any more about it, but I gave Mandy a time for her to call me. She continues the story from here.

I was thirty-two when my mother, Margaret, died. Soon after her death I started having very strange dreams. I didn't understand them and they were quite vivid and upsetting. When I saw Mandy for the first time in ages she commented on how tired I looked, and I told her what had happened. When I told her about the dreams she said I should speak to her mother as she might be able to make sense of them. Although I had known Mandy for a while, I hadn't realized that her mother was Rita Rogers.

I was terribly close to my mother. She was always there for me and we spoke every single day. Whenever I wanted any advice about the children I would go straight to her. She didn't really act like a mum in the traditional sense. She was a great friend and we would always go out together on social occasions. She was great to be around, she had this wonderful bubbly character, and we used to love going out with her in the evening. Mum really was my right arm.

Mum had died from what is known as 'industrial lung', and her passing was very unexpected and sudden. She was only fifty-three. Mum had always been quite healthy, but about three months before her death she complained of not feeling well. She had visited the doctor on several occasions and was told she had a viral infection. The doctors didn't seem too concerned about her and she was always sent home, and told that she would recover. But Mum didn't show any signs of getting better. In fact she was getting much worse and was finding it difficult to breathe. Eventually she was admitted to hospital where we were told that she had severe asthma and she was put on steroids to help her breathe.

This was a very difficult time for us. As Mum got worse they put her on more and more medication and she was heavily sedated because she was in so much pain. As if this wasn't bad enough, at regular intervals the doctors would have to stop the sedation and bring her round to see how she was. Each time they did this you could see the pain in her eyes – it was as if she was saying, 'Please stop messing with me.' She was put on a life-support machine which eventually had to be switched off.

Her death was extremely traumatic for my family. We watched a relatively young woman who had always seemed to be quite healthy slip away before us in a matter of weeks. She had gone from being a lively woman to a shadow of her former self, attached to this life-support machine. You wouldn't have put a dog through what she went through. It had all been very sudden and I think that even though we had watched her suffer so much we were shocked by her death. The very fact that she was attached to the life-support machine was traumatic enough, but then it was decided that it should be turned off and she should be allowed to die because there was nothing they could do for her. Mum had been in so much pain and was so ill that we had no choice in this matter, but it is still a terrible thing to have to go through and I wouldn't wish it on anyone.

Given how seriously ill Mum had been, I guess I should have been comforted by the fact that she was now at peace, but I wasn't really. I was extremely disturbed by the bad dreams I was having. From the moment Mum died it was as though she was trying to tell me something, although I couldn't be sure of this at the time. The dreams I was having before the reading were very traumatic and I would often wake up at night and be very anxious. I worried whether we had done the right thing by Mum, whether she was at rest, whether the doctors could have done more and so on. I was also terribly worried for my father. He had been so close to my mother that I worried what he might do now that she was gone. A reading with Rita seemed like a good idea, so I took Mandy up on her offer.

I had never had a reading before and I was quite wary of it in case I heard something bad, but Rita instantly put me at ease. She began the reading by naming other relatives who had passed over and said that they were well and happy. Then she said to me that Mum had 'died with her lungs' and then made a point of saying to me 'it wasn't cancer'. This was extremely significant. People always made the mistake of assuming that it must have been lung cancer, but 'industrial lung' is a completely different disease altogether. It is a poisoning, which we assume Mum must have got from her place of work.

During the reading Rita said that I was with my sister, which was correct, and that she was at my side. She told me that my sister had my mother's watch and that I had her ring and that I was wearing it. Again this was correct. She told me that my mother had been knitting my daughter a red cardigan but that she hadn't finished it. When Rita said this to me I knew that she wasn't faking. Mum was knitting Rebecca a red cardie before she got ill, and no, she hadn't finished it – and she wouldn't have done had she had lived. You see, it was a long-standing joke in our family that Mum never finished anything that she was knitting. So this made my sister and me laugh. Rita also talked about one of my dogs, which was due to give birth. She said she was worried about the dog and the puppies. And she was right to have been, for the dog lost the puppies later on. There was so much other stuff that Rita said too, things that no one could have known unless they were part of the family. Not even Mandy could have told her the things she was coming out with.

But the most important message was that Mum was OK and at peace and that she was well now. She said she had been in terrible pain and she was glad it was over and that we had done the right thing. She kept saying that she loved us all and that she would be there for us when we needed her. Funnily enough, I do feel her around me from time to time. There have been specific times when she has come to me when I have needed her. The small details that Rita gave us were wonderful because they backed up the one message that we all wanted to hear. She had proved to us that she was talking to my mother and that was so wonderful.

I have to be honest and admit that before the reading I wasn't a believer but Rita has changed my opinion. Rita's reading gave me such a huge amount of peace of mind. I haven't had a bad dream since the reading and that is down to her. Having watched my mother suffer so much, it meant a lot to me that she was well now, and at peace. That was all I really needed to hear.

LIFE WITHOUT A ROLE MODEL

When we are young we spend a lot of time trying not to be like our parents. We are always rebelling against what they have done and are determined not to turn out like them! This is just part of being young. It's funny, but as you get older and you start working and having a family of your own, you really begin to admire them. I sometimes wonder how on earth my parents coped. I only had four children and was a lot better off than my parents were. I can't believe how my parents managed to raise us six on what little they had and do a good job of it. You'd never hear them complain. They just got on with it. And if they went without, they never said a word about it. That was how life worked then. They dealt with each problem when it came along, and they always held their heads up high no matter what. How I admire them now.

It is really important not to take our parents for granted and to realize what an important influence they have over our lives. Of course there are times when we don't see eye to eye with them. There are moments when we might find them to be interfering or restrictive, but those moments can happen in any relationship. Getting frustrated with your parents or annoyed or irritated by them at times is completely normal, but don't underestimate the important role they play in your life. It's all too easy not to realize what you have with someone until it's too late. Sometimes it is only when you have lost something that you begin to appreciate its real worth.

We can learn a lot about life from our parents and grandparents. Not only do they have an intimate knowledge about what we are really like as people and what is best for us, but they also have the benefit of years of experience behind them. They understand just how difficult life can be and they are well aware of the struggles that we have to face to become the people we want to be.

I have said how much I loved and adored my mother and

how sad I was when she died. She really was the most wonderful woman and I admired her very much. But when I was growing up perhaps I didn't appreciate my mother as much as I could and should have done. This wasn't really her fault or mine, it had more to do with the fact that I came from such a large family. When there are lots of children in a family parents don't always have enough time to nurture and concentrate on all of their young. In my mother's case, when we were young she spent a great deal of time ill in bed because she wasn't very strong, and what time she did have was spent with the younger boys. When my little brothers came along they needed more of her time and attention and she rightly felt that my sister and I were old enough to fend, to a certain degree, for ourselves.

I was very lucky when I was growing up because I had a great bond with my paternal grandmother, Mary Alice, the Romany gypsy I inherited both my dark looks and my gift from. From the moment I was born she singled me out as her favourite. In fact I think she rather wanted me for herself! She was a formidable character and was much revered and feared in her area because of her gift, but I simply adored her. Grandma lived in Mansfield Woodhouse, a town six miles away from ours. We were so poor back then that I didn't have the bus fare to get there, but that didn't deter me. Each week I would religiously make the journey to Grandma's on foot, and it was worth it. Not only was the house full of flowers and wonderful gypsy knick-knacks but it was always warm and filled with the most wonderful smell of food cooking away on the stove. Grandma was forever baking and cooking, she'd make all sorts of wonderful things for my tea.

Once when I was in dire need of a new coat she took down

the brown dog-tooth cloth that she used as a curtain to prevent a draught from the front door and had it made into a new coat for me. That was the kind of person she was.

But that wasn't why I loved my grandmother so much. I loved being with my grandmother because she always made me feel incredibly special. At her house I wasn't one of six children – I was on my own! I didn't have to fight for attention, raise my voice to be heard or seek approval. In Grandma's house I could just be myself. Grandma always said that I had the gift, and although I didn't want to know about it when I was young because it scared me, I was always fascinated by what she did and what she knew. She would sit there by the fire and recount stories about the people she had read for and tell me all about my Romany ancestors and their beliefs. Later, when I was older, Grandma tried to encourage me to use my gift. I still wasn't sure about it at the time, but she kept on and on at me. She told me about spirit guides, and how having a gift wasn't something to be scared of – not if you used it properly. She explained how it could be used to help people.

Grandma died when I was twenty-one. She had been quite ill for a time. She was six feet tall and when she was healthy she had been nearly twenty stone; lying on her deathbed she had almost withered away. But she wasn't scared of dying. On the contrary, as a true Romany she was looking forward to it. 'What do I want down here, Rette?' she would say, laughing. 'This is your hell. You'll not get worse than this.' My father cried and cried when she went, he had loved her so. In fact he was sobbing so much and holding on to her in such a way that I thought we would never get her into the coffin. I didn't take Grandma's death so badly at the time because I thought that if she was happy then it was a good thing. But as time went on her death really began to hit me. I suddenly felt very alone without her, and longed to be able to go to her house for one of our long fireside chats.

As I began to use my gift more and more I felt increasingly lost without her. I realized that I hadn't lost just my grandmother but my mentor and role model. I had no one I could talk to about what was happening to me, no one whose advice I could seek, and that made me feel very alone. Grandma came to me from time to time in visions or as a voice in my head. She helped me gain the confidence to use my gift and was there for me as a support when really bad things happened to me. I was lucky in that way, but I still missed her support and still do. I wonder sometimes if she is proud of what I have done for people. I am sure deep down she is, because that's what she wanted for me all along. But as anyone who has lost a parent figure from his or her life will say, it would be nice to have heard it from her while she was here.

Suzanne's story

Learning to live without your parent can be very traumatic, especially if you are at a vulnerable age. Having no one to love you in that unconditional way, to treat you as though you are really special and take pride in all you do can be not only sad but actually very damaging, as the next story shows. It has been written by a young woman in Australia called Suzanne.

My mother died when I was twelve years old. I hadn't realized that she was ill. My father and my aunts and uncles had kept the information from me. When she went into hospital, before she died, I was sent to stay with an old aunt who lived miles away, so I had no idea what was going on. In fact the first I knew about Mum's condition was when my aunt called me into the sitting room and told me to pack. She said I was going home for my mother's funeral and that was that. I was the youngest child of three, but I may as well have been an only child. My older brothers were much older than me and had effectively moved away from home.

My father must have taken my mother's death badly, although I did not know this at the time. He and my mother had a very good marriage. He travelled a lot on business and my mother was very much the linchpin of the family home. She dealt with us and all our problems. Before she died we saw very little of Dad and he was not one for attending school events or anything like that. After Mum died Dad tried to be there for me to start with. He came home from work on time, he made an effort to get involved with what I was up to, but after a while he just couldn't cope. He started drinking heavily and going out a lot. I didn't realize this at the time but that was probably just his way of coping. He then threw himself into his work, started travelling a lot and I didn't really see him. It was hard for me. My brothers hardly ever came home, I spent most of my time with our neighbours and at friends' houses. I learnt about the facts of life and that sort of thing from my friends and was sent shopping for clothes with their mothers. Everyone was good to me, but I just missed my mother terribly. I had no one to talk to, no one to confide in and it hurt. I was resentful of the family life my friends had and most of all was jealous of their relationships with their mothers.

When Mum died I hadn't been given anything of hers, but about a year afterwards I went to her dressing table and took a gold locket on a chain from her jewellery box. I didn't think anyone would notice and I didn't think it was valuable. I just wanted to have something that belonged to her that I could wear close to me. If my father knew that I had taken it or indeed noticed that I was wearing it he didn't say anything.

After I left school I moved to Sydney where I got a succession of jobs, none of them leading to much. I was bright but I hadn't done well at school. I am not trying to blame everything on Mum's death, but there had been no one around to encourage me or to take pride in what I did. As I drifted from job to job I had a series of relationships, again none of them amounting to anything. I had little confidence. I went to see a therapist but that didn't seem to help much either.

In 1997 I moved in with a man who I thought I was in love with. Everything was fine at first and within a year I got pregnant. But that's when things started to go wrong. He began drinking and going out a lot. Sometimes he didn't come home for days on end. Friends told me he was seeing other women, which upset me a lot. When I put this to him he got abusive and threatened to hit me. I moved out days later and haven't seen him since. I called when our daughter was born but he wasn't interested.

Over those years I hadn't seen much of my father. He had retired from work by now and had gone to live near his family in Queensland. He had visited me a couple of times in the city and seemed to have mellowed. He hadn't asked any questions when Emily was born but he did seem to like her. To his credit he managed to remember to send her Christmas presents.

Although I hadn't had much of a relationship with my father, when my aunt called in 1999 to say that Dad had died of a heart attack I was profoundly sad. The emotion I felt rather shocked me, and quickly the sadness at losing my father became full-blown depression. For months I couldn't do anything. I could barely get myself out of bed, and if it hadn't been for Emily I don't think I would have bothered at all. I went to see a psychiatrist, who put me on some antidepressants. During our weekly meetings she suggested to me that I suffered from abandonment issues. She kept asking me if I was angry with my mother. I found this very unhelpful. How can you be angry with a woman who died of breast cancer in her forties? It wasn't her fault she died and, given the choice, I am sure that she would much rather have lived to see me grow up. If I was angry with anyone then it was with my father. But I was past blaming people; I was tired and drained and just wanted it all to end. I took myself off the medication and thought I would handle my depression on my own.

I was OK for a few months and then it hit me all over again. I was laid off from my part-time job because the company folded. It wasn't anything to do with me – I knew that deep down – but I seemed at that stage to be taking everything so personally. I felt like ending my life. As much as I loved Emily, I couldn't go on. I wasn't a good mother. I couldn't offer anything, not even financial security from my job. Surely it would be better if I was at peace? She could move on and be adopted by some nice stable family and grow up in a happy environment. I, of all people, knew how important that was.

One day I was reading a magazine and saw Rita's column. I hadn't visited a medium before and wasn't really interested in that sort of thing. The real reason I was interested in this page was because in Rita's column there was a letter from someone who was in my sort of frame of mind. The woman said she felt very low, almost suicidal, and that she had lost both her parents. Rita had managed to contact both her parents in spirit and in her reply to her she seemed to be giving this woman some good advice. I am not sure what it was about this letter, but I felt that I should write to Rita. This was something that was completely out of character for me – I had never written in to a magazine in my life before, and I had never consulted a medium. I wasn't even sure if I believed in them. Even when I went to therapy I had to be forced to go by my friends. But something was pushing me to write to Rita (I now believe that it wasn't something but someone), and so I did.

To be very honest, once I had sent the letter I put the whole thing out of my mind. In the cold light of day it seemed unlikely that Rita would ever get my letter, let alone respond to it and give me a reading. But for once, it seems, luck was on my side and in the autumn of that year I got a call saying that Rita would read for me, and an appointment was made.

I hadn't said much in the letter to Rita, only that I was very down and that I wanted to know if my mother was OK in heaven. I didn't mention any names, or when she had died, I didn't even say that I had a daughter. All I said was that I needed some guidance.

To say that Rita saved my life wouldn't be an exaggeration. At that time I was so low, had so little self-worth, so little hope in anything to do with my life that I might as well have been dead. And this sounds the most terrible thing to say, but I didn't even feel much joy in my little Emily. It was as though I was half-dead. But something amazing happened the evening that Rita read for me. It was something so incredible that within two hours I had my strength back and a sense of hope for the future.

Rita began the reading by saying that she had someone in spirit for me. Naturally I had hoped that this was my mother, but it wasn't. I was very disappointed. Rita said she had a man and she felt that he had 'gone with a bad heart'. 'Is he a John?' she asked. Rita had got my father in spirit. I cannot tell you how gutted I felt. Whilst I was amazed that so far she had got all this right, I felt cheated. Rita was saying that John, my father, was very, very sorry for neglecting me like he did. She said that he hadn't meant to hurt me and should have been a better parent. Now Rita had known nothing about my father or my upbringing, so I was amazed by what she said. She told me that my father had 'taken to the bottle' when Mum had died because he couldn't cope. 'He was very unhappy and he says he is sorry. He says he should have spent more time with you but he couldn't cope at all so he ran away from it.'

I hadn't wanted to talk to my father, I had wanted it to be Mum, but I was so moved by this, it touched such a chord. I remember that I was sitting by the phone with a glass of white wine and I had to take a huge swig from it to stop myself from crying as though I was trying to swallow my tears. 'Your father loves your little girl,' Rita said. 'He says she has your mother's name.' My mother was called Aileen. It was not a name I liked and she loathed it, so when Em was born I gave her my mother's second name – Emily. I had always liked that name, I had even called one of my dolls Emily when I was little. Rita told me that Dad was up there with my grandparents and my cousin 'Stevie', who had died in a car crash the year before. By Stevie I think Rita meant 'Stevo', who, as she said, had died the year before in a collision. I wondered whether my

*mother was going to come to me at all – the reading had gone on for
a while and I was really worried that at any moment Rita would say
'time's up' and hang up before I had spoken to her. There was no
doubt in my mind that I could speak to Mum, Rita had proved that
she was speaking to my father, but would she come? And then, just
like that, as though she was reading my mind, she said 'Your father
is bringing your mother to me.'*

*'Does her name begin with an E?' she said. Maybe she had got
it confused with Emily, I thought to myself. 'No,' I said. 'It's an E,
I'm sure. She is telling me her name is Eileen.' Eileen, the alternative
spelling for Aileen. 'She is very happy to see you she is saying, she
wants you to know how proud she is of you and how much she loves
you. She says she visits you and Emily every day. She loves Emily, she
is so proud she has her name and that she has such a lovely grandchild,' Rita said. The tears streamed down my face, falling in
puddles on my notepad where I had planned to write it all down.
But I couldn't write, my hands were shaking too much.*

*'She says she is sorry she left you and she knows you had a bad
time on your own, and if she could have been there for you she
would, but she was ill . . . was it her breast? Yes, she had cancer there,
and it killed her. She wasn't old and neither were you. You were in
your school swimming team at the time, she says.' When Rita talks
to you in a reading it's as though she is speaking to herself – by that
I mean that she doesn't expect you to say anything. Even if I had
wanted to speak I couldn't have, I was so choked. Everything Rita
told me was right. She hadn't made a single mistake and she just
rattled things off quite casually.*

*'She says you were right to take that pendant. Have you got it
on now?' I was wearing my mother's locket. 'It's a locket. She says she*

wanted you to have that, she had always meant to give it to you. But she went too quick to make arrangements. Did she have a ring? There is a small ring with blue stones – you must find that ring, that is for Emily, and you must have what is left.'

Rita told me not to worry about anything. She said that my parents were proud of me and especially proud of Emily. She said that Mum knew that I was drifting but that I would find my way. She said that I had been involved with a man called Rob. This was the name of Emily's father. She said that Mum didn't like him at all and she was sorry that it had ended badly for my sake, but that it was good that it was over, as he would have caused me more pain. She said that Rob drank heavily and that Rita felt that he did drugs too. Months after I left Rob I discovered that he had been taking heroine throughout our relationship. I hadn't known about it – he had hidden it from me, which can happen.

Rita said that Mum was telling her that she was sending someone for me. She said that I already knew him but she felt I hadn't seen him for some time. She gave me the initial 'P'. She said he drove a red car and that he worked with people. She said he would be my soulmate and that he would be a father to Emily.

Rita said the city wasn't good for me and that I needed more open space. She said that before I met the 'P' I would have to sort my life out. She said she saw me working with young children and that this would make me happy. 'You have so much to live for, you mustn't do anything silly,' she said, quite matter-of-factly. These were the main points of my reading. Rita said a lot more to me but these were the things that stood out and in effect changed my life. After the reading I sat on my bed for a while and tried to get my head round everything that Rita had said to me. For the first time in *months I felt like I could breathe. This weight had been lifted from me, I no longer felt suffocated. I took a deep breath and exhaled and as I hugged my pillow I thought about my future.*

I think that my problems came from the fact that I had no self-worth. Of course a lot of that had to do with work and a succession of bad relationships, which were all of my doing. Whether these problems wouldn't have happened had Mum not died or Dad been around for me more I can't say for sure, but what I do know is that you can't underestimate the effect your parents have on your life. Had my mother been alive to encourage me more, or to advise me, or even to support me, I think things would have been different in the sense that I might have coped better with each problem. After I had left Rob, rather than feeling totally isolated and abandoned in this world it would have been good if I had been able to turn to my parents for love and support. But life isn't always like that. I know that now.

Some months after the reading I gave up the lease on my small apartment in the city and moved back to the suburb where I had grown up. I thought this sensible as I had friends there. For the price of my one-bedroom apartment I have a two-bedroom bungalow with an outside space where Em can play. Being part of a community has been good for me. I have my friends and their mothers, the ones who cared for me when I was a child, who love Em and are great babysitters. Because of that I was able to get some part-time work. I have a position at the local school which Em attends working as an assistant in the office. It suits me perfectly. In my first month there I met Peter. We had been at high school together and he works in the area now as a community worker. We weren't great friends at school because we were in different groups, but we have got to know each other again and have started dating. He is divorced and has a two-year-old son called Ben. Is this the 'P' my mother sent me? Who knows, it's early days, but it feels nice.

I visited my mother's sister in June and asked her if she had Mum's jewellery box. She said she did. She had meant to give it to me years ago but I think that she was frightened that I might go and pawn the lot. In fact there wasn't anything of any real value in it, but there was something there that did mean a lot to me and is worth more than money. It's a small gold ring with tiny aquamarine stones in a cluster. It's much too small for my fingers and anyway it wasn't meant for me. But I wear it next to my mother's locket on a chain around my neck, and when Em is old enough I will give it to her.

My reading with Rita didn't bring Mum back to me, and it didn't give me back my childhood either, but what it did give me was hope for a future. I know now that whilst Mum and Dad aren't here for me physically, they are here for me in other ways. I wouldn't want to take my own life now, I have no need to, but my main reason is that I don't want Emily to grow up without a parent. My reading showed me that and gave me faith to live again.

7. Losing a Friend

We don't choose our family but we do choose our friends, which is why it is so sad when we lose them from our lives. Friendship is one of the most precious gifts there is in life. A true friend, one you really love and trust, is a rarity. You can have a great many acquaintances and be very popular, but finding someone you can call a real friend isn't so easy. We spend a lifetime searching for people that we get on well with, who we gel with, people to share our highs and our lows with. These are the people we turn to when we cannot talk to our families or soulmates, the people we share our secrets with and confide in. The ones we turn to when no one else will listen, and the ones we have some of the happiest times of our lives with. So when we lose a friend we lose a great deal from our lives. And because our friends say so much about who we are as an individual, we lose a small part of our identity too.

A common assumption people mistakenly make is that we grieve only for those that have been either related to us or married to us. When we think of someone who dies we immediately feel sympathy for their immediate family, their children and husband or wife. Rarely do we consider the feelings of their great friends or wonder what effect this death is having on their lives. We don't take compassionate leave from work when our best friend dies, nor do we receive sympathy cards or letters of condolence, because when it comes to loss, people naturally think first about the family's mourning, grief and pain.

And yet true friendship is a very special thing and quite often that relationship can be much stronger than anything we might have with our own families. We choose our friends for a reason. Initially we form these relationships because we are compatible, because we have the same outlook and share the same interests, but as time goes on that relationship becomes stronger and intensifies until we find ourselves in a relationship where we are sharing not just good times, but confidences and secrets besides. Words such as loyalty and trust come into play. We begin to share things that we wouldn't necessarily tell our family, not because we don't like them, but because often that relationship is just too complicated.

The wonderful thing about friends is that they take us as we are. With our friends we can be ourselves. We are who we truly are without the trappings of family bonds. With them we aren't a wife, mother, sister or daughter. We aren't a husband, father, brother or son. We can just be who we are, and sometimes that can be very refreshing.

I read quite a lot for people who have lost friends. This surprises many people because they assume that people who visit mediums or want to contact their loved ones in spirit must be family members, but people who assume this are missing the point – you can have just as much love for a friend as you do for a member of your own family. When your friend dies you can feel just as much pain as is if they were related to you.

Because we assume that family members are the ones who suffer the most when a person dies, friends often get sidelined or forgotten in the grieving process, and as a result of this friends can often feel terribly isolated in their pain. If you think about it, when a member of your family dies you have people to turn to, people who understand what you are going through and what that person meant to you. This is a time when families come together, lean on each other and unite in their loss and through their bond. But the *friend* of the person who has passed away doesn't have this framework or support system. Your spouse, mother or father might understand how close you were to your friend, but do they really understand the hole that has been created in your life? Do they know how much you really miss them? Do they understand what the two of you shared? Probably not, because friendships are often very private relationships.

I am never surprised when people come to me for readings with their friends who have passed over because I think this is often the only outlet for their grief. Being excluded from the family framework, they need someone else to talk to about their loss and how this has affected them. More importantly, given the fact that they have lost their best friend, they are always very keen to be able to communicate with them once again. Friendship is a close bond that we choose to make, not one we are forced to make through blood ties, so the communication we have with a friend can be far more intimate than the communication we have with our own family, especially since not all of us have close links with our families and some don't have families at all. And for those who have not found their soulmate the relationship with their friend may be the closest and most important relationship they have. In situations such as these, the death of a friend can be absolutely devastating.

We have many different sorts of friends in our lives. There are those we have known since childhood or from early on in our lives, who we share a lot of history with. Then there are those who we meet later on in life, who we have something major in common with, perhaps doing the same job or sharing the same hobby. And finally there are the friends who on the face of it we have little in common with, people we don't spend that much time with and yet with whom we share a very strong bond. Whatever kind our friend is, the fact is that when they die we are left with a very empty place in our lives.

PETS

For some people the death of a pet can be just as traumatic and heartbreaking as the death of a human being. Poeple who have never owned a pet may scoff at such a thought, but anyone who has ever really loved an animal will understand what I am talking about. We shouldn't underestimate the feelings people have for their pets and we should realize that this sense of loss can be heartbreaking. Owning a pet is a huge commitment, we spend a great deal of time caring for our animals, walking them, feeding them, making sure they are in good health and are happy. In return, they give us love and companionship and they become part of the family. Because of this, for many people, especially those who are on their own, the relationship they have with their pet is an extremely close one. They may well spend more time with their pet than they do with anyone else.

So when a pet dies people often find they are left with a

terrible hole in their lives. They grieve for the loss of companionship their pet gave them. They miss the routine they had caring for their pet and they miss having something to love. There is something very vulnerable about a pet, which is why we mind so much when they get hurt or are sick; we don't like to see them suffer in any way. I am a great dog lover and I know that every time we have lost a dog I have been deeply saddened and have grieved.

What I want people who have lost animals to realize is that when they pass away they also go to the spirit world. We are all God's creatures and so when we die we *all* go on into the after life. I know this is true because so often when I am reading for people I am able to tell them about their pets who have passed over. I will picture their dog, cat, horse and so on and will be able to describe them. The other thing to point out here is just as our loved ones are able to visit us from the spirit world so too do the spirits of our pets. I often see the spirit of my beloved collie Lassie out in our garden, and though I miss her very much I am very comforted by the knowledge that when my time comes I will be reunited with her.

LIFELONG FRIENDS

I always think that we are quite lucky if we still have the same friends we had when we were young. Most people drift apart from the friends that they had when they were little – they either grow apart or they end up moving away and losing contact. The friendships we make when we are tiny or at school are probably not the people we might choose to be our friends when we grow older. When we are very young we are less selective about people, and friendships are forged on the thinnest of common denominators – we might make friends because we go to the same school, because we live locally, because our parents are friends, for instance. And yet, that said, these friendships can be surprisingly strong. If you think about it, you have a long shared personal history, and that rather innocent bond that you formed as a child can take you through the rest of your life.

Similarly, the friendships you have as young adults can be equally rewarding. The first friends that you 'choose' are made with few conditions. It's not about anyone else, just about you two. These are the friends you make as you are just beginning to experience life, and these shared experiences give you a great common ground that grows stronger as you develop. Whether you meet in the cradle, in the crèche or at college, these are the people I call 'lifelong friends' because that is what you share – your lives. And though you might move on, or move away and even lose complete contact, I believe that these friends always stay with you in some way. There is always a place in your heart for these people because you have shared so much of your formative years together. So when a lifelong friend dies, it's hard for us because when we bury them we bury part of our past as well.

I was very young when I first got pregnant with Pat, my eldest daughter. My husband and I knew we needed a bigger place with a family on the way, and so we moved to Victoria Street in Mansfield. The two-up two-down was our first proper house and I was so excited. Dennis had worked hard to get the deposit together and we wondered how on earth we were going to pay the mortgage, which was £5 a month. Victoria Street was only a few miles from my family, but I didn't have a car, so I was hoping that I might meet some nice people in our street. As luck would have it, next door but one lived a woman called June who quickly became my best friend.

June was Irish. She was married to a man called Joe and we hit it off straight away. We became firm friends and did everything together, from the shopping to helping each other out. We were so close we were pretty much like sisters. It helped that our husbands liked each other too. Joe played the accordion and we had some pretty wild nights together.

Things were not good financially in those days, so June and I learned to share everything we had between us. Every morning we would have coffee together and we would take it in turns to buy the cakes or biscuits. During these coffee mornings she and I would discuss everything from domestic matters of little importance to our marriages and how we felt about life. June had worked as a nurse, looking after disabled children. She got me a job where she worked, which I loved. We were, to be honest, pretty much inseparable. June was with me when I gave birth to all my girls, because I had them at home. I was there for her when she had to go to hospital for a hysterectomy. As our kids were more or less the same ages, they would play together, and when one of us was busy the other would keep on eye on the children. When my marriage went through a bad patch, June was the only person I could confide in.

We eventually moved house to Newton Street as the family got bigger, but June and I still kept in touch daily, meeting in

Mansfield or visiting each other. By now we were firm friends, so much so that I named my youngest, Kerry June, after her. She was thrilled. She really was my best friend, and I would have trusted her with my life. I could tell her things that I would never dare bring up with my husband, my parents or even my own siblings, and she felt the same. She was there for me the night before Pat got married (we got terribly drunk making sherry trifles and into terrible trouble with our husbands), and she was also there for me when Dennis died.

When I met Mo we moved to Skegness and so I was quite far away from June. I think this was one of the reasons that I never really felt comfortable there at that time. June had become so much part of the fabric of my life that I wasn't happy being so far away from her. I felt that part of me was missing when I was there. We moved back to Mansfield eventually, but five years had passed and the sad truth was that June and I had drifted apart. It wasn't anything to do with each of us on a personal level; it had more to do with geography.

I will never forget the day that Pat rang me and told me the sad news. She said that someone had died, but before she even got a chance to tell me who it was I had guessed. I knew straight away, she didn't have to tell me. I felt absolutely terrible. My first reaction was to call Joe, but there was no reply. I knew that they hadn't moved from their old house, so I kept trying. Eventually I found Joe's brother's number and spoke to him. He said that Joe had passed away a few months before June.

To hear that two such good friends had gone upset me deeply, and all the memories came flooding back. We had all been so much part of each other's lives for so long. But the worst thing about June's death was that I felt I had let her down and I felt very guilty about that. She could have done with my support, just as she had always been there for me. Even if I had simply been there to hold her hand, that would have been enough. I was devastated and heartbroken but, most of all, furious with myself. I still feel June around me. I can see her in my mind and hear her wonderful lilting Irish accent telling me 'Away with you, Rita!' It is sad that we lost touch, but I am still grateful that for thirty-five years I had a truly wonderful friend, and I do miss her like mad.

Joanne's story

Sometimes the death of a lifelong friend can be as traumatic for us as the death of a brother or sister, particularly if we have grown up together. Not so long ago I read for a girl called Joanne who had lost her best friend Alan. Alan and Joanne had been friends since they were tiny babies and had grown up together. When Alan died Joanne was devastated by the loss of her friend and came to me for a reading.

Before the reading began I didn't know who Joanne had lost. She was obviously quite upset and so I had assumed that she must have lost a family member or perhaps a boyfriend. But once the reading started and Alan came through, as clear as a bell, I realized that she had lost a great, great friend. There was such a feeling of love between these two that I wasn't surprised she had been so upset.

Alan began the reading by telling me that he was with his

mother, Olive, and his father, Joe. Alan told me that he was gay and that he wanted Joanne to know that his parents were fine about his sexuality now. This had been something that had obviously bothered him when he was growing up and he had confided to Joanne his fears of coming out to his parents. He was such a character during the reading. He had this wonderful feminine voice and he wouldn't draw breath!

He was telling me that while he was alive he was obsessed about his weight and that he was always immaculately dressed and well turned out. Alan said that for many years he had struggled with his sexuality and had tried to be straight for the sake of his parents, but he explained that this had been very hard for him because he had fallen in love with Peter, his partner for many years. Alan said he wanted Joanne to tell his friend David how much he missed him and wanted to thank him for taking so much care of him while he was very ill.

Then Alan began to show me a picnic scene and was telling me how he and Joanne would go for day trips together. As he was telling me this I had this very warm feeling. I felt that this was when the two of them had been really happy. Alan told me that Joanne's parents were friends with his parents and that he was there with Joanne's dad, Joe, in spirit. He told me that Joanne was an only child and that her dad called her his princess.

During the reading I was struck by just how close Joanne and Alan were. He was telling me that he was the brother that Joanne never had. He told me that he visited Joanne every couple of days and in order to prove this he talked to me about Joanne's husband Michael, who he said he liked very much, and her two children Joseph and Lorna. He also spoke about

Joanne's friends Chris and Steven, who were also in spirit, and told me about his funeral and who was there.

Alan wanted to get in touch with Joanne because he knew that she had taken his death very badly. He said that he had been trying hard to let her know that he was now OK. I am sure this was the case as over the weeks before this reading I am certain that I had picked Alan up, although at the time I wasn't sure who he was connected to. Alan really wanted Joanne to know that he would always be a friend to her even though he had passed over. Alan still loved Joanne very much and knew how much she loved him as a friend and surrogate brother. The last thing he said to me in the reading was that he would never leave Joanne and that he would always be at her side and watching out for her.

What this reading proved to me is that even though our friends die they never stop being our friends and loving us, and although we can no longer see or hear them that does not mean that they are not there for us every step of the way.

COMPANION FRIENDS

Companion friends are the friends we meet later on in our lives. Unlike the lifelong friend, the companion friend is not someone you have known since childhood or met when you were quite young. These are people you meet once you have grown up and become the kind of person you are today. Whilst you share a history and a social life with your lifelong friend, you don't with your companion friend. What you share is an interest or an outlook that defines you both as individuals and it is this that bonds you together. They might, for example, be someone you met through your work, or through one of your hobbies. They could be someone you met when you were studying or even later on in life when you had both retired.

You may not socialize with your companion friend, you may keep them quite separate from your day-to-day life, but the link that you have between you is incredibly strong. Because of this bond you can often go for months without seeing each other, but when you do meet again that friendship is just as intense as it was when you left off. This person is not someone you have to make small talk with, have over to dinner parties or even have to introduce to your family and friends, for your very personal and deep friendship does not depend on social situations for its existence.

Because you share such a deep friendship and because this friend exists on a separate level of your life, you often find yourself sharing a great many things with this person that you would be unable to talk to either your family or lifelong friends about. The companion friend is a true friend, one who takes you as you are, and is loyal, trustworthy and honest. And because of all this, when they do pass over before us we are left with a huge void in our lives. One that can't ever be filled by another person, no matter how wonderful they are.

My companion friend was a woman called Jean. Doing what I do for a living, it is hard to find people who actually understand what I do and are able to offer support and advice. At one stage I felt very isolated because of my work and got very depressed. After all, this isn't the kind of profession where you can meet after work, have a drink and moan about the boss! All that changed when, in 1982, I met the wonderful Jean while I was living in

Skegness. Mo and I were running a guest house, but I was still reading for people full-time. Jean had booked an appointment for a reading and from the moment I opened the door to her I knew that there was something about her that was special.

Jean was a little older than me and wore her hair in a beehive. There was nothing extraordinary about her appearance, but I could tell that she was different. One psychic always knows another, and I could tell at just a glance that she was very spiritual. It was something about her composure and her manner. I sat down and began to read for her. When I was halfway through the reading, she interrupted me and said, 'While you have been reading me, I have been reading you.' I wasn't that surprised by this – as I said, I knew this woman was different – but when she asked me who Dennis was I nearly fell off my chair. For once the tables were being turned on me. Since my Romany grandmother had passed away, no one had ever given me a proper reading. I was also taken aback because no one had ever contacted my husband before. Yes, I had spoken to him myself and in times of despair and distress I had felt his presence around me, but it wasn't like this.

Jean was married and lived in Sheffield. She had two daughters and worked with old people. Although Jean had incredible psychic powers, she did not do private sittings. She kept her gift to herself, but I have to say that she bowled me over with the reading she gave me that day. From that moment we bonded. At last I had found someone who shared my gift, someone who could understand what I did, and how hard it was at times. And I do believe that she was sent to me for that reason. Being a medium can be an exceptionally lonely job. It's not like you have colleagues. Most people don't understand what I do, and so it was a relief to at last find someone who did.

And so our friendship began. Often we didn't see each other for a year, but that didn't matter – when we did meet it was as though I had been with her only the day before. She always knew when to call – one of the great things about having a psychic as a friend, I suppose. Whenever I was very down, she would call me. And if I had a bad day reading, I would telephone her and she would understand exactly why I was upset or why the reading hadn't gone so well.

My friend Rose called one day to say that she felt she had a spirit in her new house. The spirit was up to all sorts of mischief and Rose was, quite understandably, terrified. 'Please come and sort it out for me, Rita,' she begged. Now Jean was always one for saying that psychics must be wary of bad spirits and put protection round themselves. This would involve asking a spirit guide for help, or making sure that you were with another person with psychic abilities when you confronted the bad spirit. There is always the danger that a bad spirit might not want to ascend, might want to attach themselves to the medium or, worse still, do them some harm. The afternoon I went to see Rose, I didn't take any of these precautions. I was in a hurry and didn't think that it could be too serious there.

When I arrived at the house I have to say that at once I felt nervous of this spirit, but I made contact with him and asked him to leave Rose alone, which he agreed to. When I got home later on I felt awful, really sick. I was breathless and weak and I had no idea what was wrong with me. As far as I was aware I was physically very ill, I didn't think it could be anything else, but just before I took myself off to bed for a rest I called Jean. 'Oh, Rita,' she said, as I explained how bad I felt. 'You have only gone and brought that spirit home with you. It may have promised to leave Rose alone, but it's attached itself to you.' Jean managed to exorcize the spirit from me and as soon as that was done I felt better.

On another occasion I was bedridden following a bad fall. I was semi-concussed and was almost delirious as I lay there in bed. All the time I was ill I could feel spirits around me. I could recognize most of them, but there was one lady who kept appearing to me but whom I did not know. All I knew about her was her name: Mary. Sensing I wasn't well, Jean called Mo, who told her what had happened, and she came straight away to be with me. She sat down by my bed and told me that there was a lady there with us and that she had come to take care of me. She said that her name was Caroline. She described her to me as being large with a cuddly frame, and said that she was wearing a hairnet and black beads. She was describing the woman I had seen, but I couldn't understand this, as the woman I had seen had told me her name was Mary. Later that afternoon my mother came to visit and I told her about the visions Jean and I had seen. When I described the woman to her, Mum burst into tears and said, 'That's my mother!' I hadn't met my maternal grandmother because she had died before I was born. I asked why she had told Jean that her name was Caroline, and Mum told me that her real name was Caroline Mary but everyone in our family just called her Mary. Mum also told me that she had been praying to her mother to help me get better.

My friendship with Jean continued like this over the years

and I was very grateful that I had someone like her in my life. It's funny, but when you do what I do and spend your life helping other people, there are very few people who can actually do the same for you. Countless times I have been able to make sense of the madness of other people's lives, help them understand what their dreams are about, or give them the strength to confront their fears and problems, but when it comes to my own life it's not so easy. Unfortunately, mediums can't read for themselves. But just as I was able to help Jean, she was able to help me. Together we made a good team.

My family and close friends have always been a great support to me and have come to accept what I do and to understand it, but I think it's still very hard for them to truly know what it is like to work as a medium. I was lucky to have Jean in my life because she filled that hole. She was able to help me in so many ways, whether it was to warn me off people, to help me understand visions or voices from the spirit world or even simply to be there at the other end of the telephone after a long day of readings.

I was devastated when Jean's daughter called me to say that she had died. I felt for a moment as though I was suddenly all alone in the world once again. But that feeling did not last long, for if there was one person I knew who would be able to get in touch with me after they had died, it was going to be Jean! Within days of her passing she was in my ear, passing messages on to her daughter about what she wanted for her funeral and so forth. When I get very down with work or depressed by the readings I have given, then I turn to Jean for a chat. I miss her terribly and often wish she was sat here in front of me, giving me advice or just talking. But I am lucky because even though she isn't physically here, I do know that she is here with me in spirit watching out for me and that she has become my self-appointed guardian angel.

KARMIC FRIENDS

Just as spirits send us soulmates they also send us friends to help us through life and these people are called 'karmic friends'. Karmic friends are the people with whom we share a spiritual link. We all have a blueprint for our lives that sets out our destiny and that destiny also holds people we are supposed to meet. Karmic friends are people with whom we share a special bond. On the face of it you might have nothing in common with this person. They may be from a completely different background. You could even be polar opposites. Yet there is something about this person which you are deeply attracted to. And so you form a friendship which no one else can understand. I am talking here about being more than just good friends. These are people with whom you can share very special and intimate details and thoughts – things you couldn't share with anyone else – because they will understand you.

These are the friends who have been sent to you by the spirit world. As a result you may not have met through the usual channels but may have met in an unusual place or in an unusual way. You may have known them only for five minutes but already it feels like a lifetime. Because of the spiritual link between you you have a deep understanding of the other person.

There is an intuition between you. You instinctively know how your friend is feeling, you are sensitive to each other's needs. You trust each other implicitly. Other people you know might not understand how you are feeling, but you can always rely on your karmic friend to know what you are going through. These are the friends who help you out in life, who enlighten you, who take you for who you are and as you are. They have nothing but respect for you and never judge you because the relationship you have is based on a spiritual connection.

I was introduced to Diana, later the Princess of Wales, by a mutual friend back in 1994. Diana had always been a very spiritual person. Because of her position and who she was, I think she was always searching for meaning in her life. And because of her charity work, Diana had come face to face with a great deal of suffering and so she needed to find comfort and meaning in the tragedies that she witnessed. Some of her critics have suggested that Diana played to the media and that her charity work was just part of an act, but anyone who knew her well would dispute this argument. She cared a great deal about her charity work and would tirelessly campaign for a cause she believed in, but she found it difficult. She needed to make sense of it all, she needed to believe that there was more to life and that these people would one day find peace and happiness.

Our mutual friend had been coming to readings with me for a couple of years and would often talk to Diana about them. Diana was curious; although she didn't fully believe in what I was doing at the time, nevertheless she thought that she would like to talk to me and so our friend arranged a telephone reading for her. That's how it all began. As time passed she began to call more regularly – sometimes as often as every other day. Sometimes she would call for a reading, sometimes she would ring to see how I was or for a chat. Diana spent a great amount of time on her own. She would do her charity work during the day but when she came home at night, with her boys away at school she would be on her own, having had her supper in front of the telly, so often she would pick up the phone and call me knowing that I rarely go out in the evenings. She would talk about her work, what she had seen, the people she had met and what effect that had had on her. Sometimes she spoke about how she was, other times she just wanted a chat and a gossip about what I was up to. I guess she just needed a friend to speak to.

I said that we often spoke on the telephone but it took a whole year before I met her in person. Understandably, she had to know she could trust me. When she did arrive at my house having driven the whole way from London herself, I remember feeling very nervous, but from the moment she literally bounced into my house, those nerves were forgotten. She was not the princess from the television, the one I saw in magazines or newspapers. She was a down-to-earth, friendly girl, a very pretty young English woman with a heart of gold and a mischievous sense of humour.

What I liked about Diana was that there were no airs and graces with her. In my line of work you get to read for a great many famous people. To be honest, I am not fazed by any of them. (Usually I don't even know who they are till they tell me!) The fact is, I'm not really bothered whether someone is in a rock band, has been on the television or in a film. The people who matter to me are the ones who have had problems, suffered tragedies, lost their kids and so on. And I am not impressed when someone in that position uses their fame to 'jump the queue' or demand readings when it suits them. But with Diana it was different. Yes, she was the most famous young woman in the world at that time, yes, she was mother to the future king of England, and yes, I was apprehensive when I met her because I wondered what she would make of my house, having lived in a palace for so long. But when she was sat there on my sofa that first afternoon in her jeans, munching chocolates and bananas and chatting away to me, she could have been one of my daughters' friends who had stopped in for a cup of tea. She went round the house looking at all my things and going into all the rooms, and I remember apologizing to her for my home. 'It's not a palace,' I mumbled, quite embarrassed. And you know what, she looked me straight in the eye and said to me, 'No, but it's you, Rita, and I love it!' And she really meant it.

From that afternoon Diana and I forged the most unlikely of friendships. She was the Princess of Wales, she had been born into a good family, was young, beautiful, rich and famous. I was a fifty-something medium, born to working-class parents and descended from Romany gypsy folk. But deep down we had more in common than people could imagine. We shared the same star sign, Cancer, for a start, so our reactions to things were similar. Cancer signs can be great fighters on the outside but deep down they are extremely sensitive people who need to be loved. Because of this I understood what made Diana happy and what made her sad or angry. Also, we were both mothers and great believers in the importance of family, always putting our children first. She and I had both had difficult upbringings. We shared the same sense of humour and outlook on life. But I think the most significant thing that brought us together as kindred spirits was the work that we did. Diana enjoyed her charity work but found it harrowing at times because of the suffering she saw. My vocation is to read for people, but I often find it emotionally very draining. Both of us found it difficult to switch off at night from what we had been through during the day, and so we found comfort and solace in our evening chats.

Diana and I were not people who would have socialized together or met through our work or through our backgrounds. Yet that is not to say that our friendship wasn't strong and deep. She had a great gift for seeing the world as other people see it, which is why she was so popular and was described at the time of her death as the 'people's princess'. She didn't mind the fact that I came from another background – if anything I think she thought it gave me a freedom that she didn't have. At the time of her death (and still to this day), I was approached by the press to talk about her readings and was offered thousands of pounds to do so. Whilst I am happy to talk about what a wonderful friend she was to me I would never stoop so low, and such offers caused me great offence. I would never 'sell' anyone's reading to anyone, whoever they were. Readings are intensely private and I would not talk about anything that was said behind my doors unless I had permission to do so. But there is another reason why I wouldn't sell Diana out, and that is because she and I both believed in loyalty and trust. That is what friendship is all about, after all.

When she died I was profoundly sad about her death, especially because she was so young, and I felt so sorry for her children. But looking back I am pleased that she is now at peace and can be the free spirit she always craved to be.

WHEN FAMOUS PEOPLE DIE

You don't necessarily have to have known someone personally to grieve for them when they die. Often we get terribly upset when someone in the limelight passes away. The public outpouring of grief displayed when the late Princess of Wales died is a good example of this. Hundreds of thousands of people who had not even met the princess felt terribly upset by her passing. Round the world people had vigils for her. In the United Kingdom, even people who were far from being royalist queued for hours to sign books of condolence, and thousands lined the streets to pay their respects on the day of her funeral. I received many letters around this time from people who were upset by her tragic death. Many wanted to know why they felt the way they did given that they did not even know her. One lady who wrote to me said that she didn't even particularly like the princess when she was alive but was so moved by her death that she couldn't stop crying. 'Why do I feel this way, Rita? she asked.

My answer to this is straightforward: you don't have to have met someone to feel that you have known him or her. We all knew Diana in our own way. She grew up in full view of the public. We shared her joys, her sadness – much of her life. Because of the way she connected with the general public, she did have a very special place in a lot of people's hearts. The same could be said of the late Queen Mother.

But there is another reason why we felt the death of Diana so greatly and that is because she died young. There is nothing more tragic than a life cut short. It haunts us all, and is the reason why the deaths of people like President Kennedy, Marilyn Monroe, Princess Grace or Jill Dando also affected people so much. When someone dies young and in tragic circumstances we are shocked and react quite strongly to this news, even remembering exactly where we were when we were told of their deaths. Our hearts go out not just for the person who has lost their life, but also for their families. Who can forget the image of Jackie Kennedy in her blood-stained dress, or the sight of the young Princes William and Harry walking behind their mother's coffin? Even if you were not a great fan of these people you could not help but be moved by these deaths. This sense of loss and grief is contagious and spreads to us all.

Because these people have touched our lives, we grieve for them and their families. We are showing signs of sympathy and empathy. We may not have known them but we feel their families' pain and we mourn the loss of their presence in our lives.

Pat's story

The loss of a karmic friend can upset us just as much as the death of a soulmate. Because the connection we have with our karmic friend is incredibly spiritual, when we lose them from our lives we lose part of our souls too. We feel that loss from deep within us and when they die we really miss the 'connection' we had made with them. The following story is about Pat, who lost her karmic friend not so long ago. Although their relationship was not sexual or romantic, when Pat lost her doctor friend she suffered intensely. When she called me for a reading I was at first slightly confused for the love I felt existed between these two souls was so warm and intense that I imagined, to begin with, that perhaps they were soulmates. But as the reading went on I realized that in fact they were karmic friends. Both had a soulmate of their own, yet this did not diminish in any way the love that they had for each other or the intensity of grief that poor Pat felt when she lost her friend. Here she tells the story in her own words:

When I received the phone call from Rita, it came at a time when I was feeling very low because some friends had just moved and I had been very attached to them, especially the children, who were very close to my heart. It hurts a lot when you lose a friend, be it by moving or by death.

I lost another dear friend some years ago. He was a doctor whom I got to know over a six-year period and eventually we became close friends. One day, nearly three years ago, I was due to see him but he never arrived. I was extremely worried when he didn't show up because it was so out of character, so I left a note for him asking him to call me. But he never did. The following day when I rang his home, his friends answered to say that he had died sometime the day before. They had found my note and had called the caretaker to let them in.

I felt angry and shocked but mostly guilty for not doing anything about it the day before. I kept thinking that I should have rung the police for them to check he was OK.

In the early hours of the next morning I awoke to see a figure of a man dressed casually. He was smiling and walking across from the corner of my room. At first I thought that I must be dreaming, and then I realized that I wasn't and that it was my friend Jonathan. It was as though he was trying to tell me something, but I didn't know what it was.

One day I heard a medium talking on the radio. It was a phone-in and although I wanted to talk to someone about what had happened I thought it was much too public for me to call in – I didn't want that. Then I came across a book written by Rita, called From One World to Another. *Finding her address in the book, I wrote to her and asked her for a reading. She wrote back and made an appointment for a telephone reading.*

The first person to come through in the reading was my mother who had died when I was just eight and a half, nearly fifty years ago. Then my sister Barb came through who had died eight years before. They both sent me their love. Then Jonathan came through. He sent me all his love and was telling Rita that we were companion soulmates and said that we would be reunited in the next life.

Rita said that he wanted me to send myself a dozen red roses, which meant love always from him. This was very appropriate and he would have known that this meant a great deal to me. He also told Rita that I had the ability to heal people and that I should do something about this gift.

I found Rita to be a genuine and caring person and the reading really helped me a lot. It meant a lot to me that my mother had come to me. She had suffered a great deal on earth and it was good to know that she was now OK. She had been the most loving and caring mother anyone could have wished for. It was also good to know that my dear sister was happy and back in the arms of my mother, whom she had missed so much. But I think what really mattered to me at that time was that Jonathan was happy and now at peace. And I have found that true friendship from a mother, sister or a friend will live on for ever in your heart no matter where they are.

8. *Losing a Soulmate*

Our soulmate is the person to whom we are spiritually linked. Between you and your soulmate exists an immutable force of attraction, one that goes beyond anything that we might have felt for another person in the past or indeed in the future. It is an attraction that you feel from deep inside you. Looks, sexuality, class, age, background all become irrelevant because the love you have for each other comes not just from the heart but from the soul itself. Your soulmate is the person you were destined to be with when your soul was conceived. As a result, your soulmate – alongside your children with whom you share an equally special bond – is the most important person in your life.

Your soulmate is not just your lover but your companion, the one you depend on, rely on and live for. Your soulmate is your best friend; the one who shapes your life, rocks your world, gives you the reason to live; the one who looks beyond everything else and loves you for who and what you really are. And from this deep and totally unconditional love comes an understanding that you will never know with another person. The love our soulmate gives us and we return enriches us and gives us meaning. It is a love that makes us feel whole, one that brings us joy and happiness. It is the deepest and most profound of all loves.

We are all destined to have a soulmate. Whether we meet them in this life or the next each of us has a special person to whom we are spiritually linked and destined to be with. When we lose our soulmate we lose the person to whom we are closest. We lose the person who has given us faith in both life and love; the one who gave meaning and purpose to our life; the one who brought light into the darkness, gave us comfort when we were down, strength when we were weak, made us laugh when we were sad and, above all, understood us.

We spend most of our life searching for our soulmate in the belief that once we have found them our life will feel complete, happy and fulfilled. We spend much of our life preparing to meet them. We imagine when we are younger what that love will feel like and who our soulmate will be. We imagine what our first meeting will be like, when this love affair will begin. Once we have met, we fantasize about our future life together. We might imagine what our wedding and marriage will be like, whether we will have children, being together in old age. For this is the person whom we recognize we are destined to be with.

But what happens to you when destiny forces you and your soulmate to be apart? It is quite ironic that we devote so much of our lifetime preparing to be with our soulmate, yet give so little thought to what our life would be like without them.

I lost my husband Dennis to cancer. We had been together for twenty years. My Romany grandmother had predicted that I would marry young and at the age of sixteen I eloped with Dennis Rogers, who was a fitter in the coal mines. I can't say that it was love at first sight, but there was something about this man that made me feel secure. He was twenty-four and had good prospects. He also wanted to take care of me, make a life with me, and as my father started to become increasingly possessive of me as I grew up, the idea of starting a new life became more and more appealing. Of course marriage didn't make life any easier for us, and for years Dennis and I struggled. Money was short, times were hard then and we both worked long hours. It was the birth of our four daughters that I think cemented our love and by the time my youngest, Kerry, was born there was nothing that could come between our close family unit. Or so I thought.

Just as my grandmother predicted I would marry young and have four daughters, she also predicted that I would be widowed young. After her death she came to me in a vision and said, 'Dennis will die soon, Rette. When the roses die, Dennis will die too.' I was filled with an overwhelming sense of sadness when I heard this. My grandmother had been correct with all the predictions she had made about my life over the years, and I didn't doubt she was right, but the fact is I had known that Dennis was not long of this world for quite some time. For months he had been quite ill and I knew that he would die within the year. Dennis's condition deteriorated over that summer. He lost weight, was gaunt-looking and his stomach had swollen. He was sent to hospital for tests and on Friday the thirteenth, of all days, I was called in to see the doctor and told he had two months to live. 'Two months.' It was midsummer. In two months my roses would be dead and so too would the husband whom I adored.

Even though I had been prepared for his death thanks to my grandmother's prediction and the doctor's diagnosis, nothing could have prepared me for the grief I would go through after-wards. My belief in the afterlife had enabled me to rationalize what had happened. I knew that Dennis, who had suffered so much at the hands of his cancer, was in a better place now. And thanks to my gift I was able to communicate with him. The visions I had of him soon after his death when he visited me were of a man in his prime, the fifteen-stone man I knew, not the six-stone shell he was when he died, a man without pain, a man who was happy and above all at peace. But even with this knowledge I was broken. You see, the grief I was suffering then was not for Dennis but – and this may sound selfish – for myself.

In the months and years that followed I was haunted by sadness. Remember that I had spent the whole of my adult life with Dennis. I was a very young mother of four daughters. I had to carry on for them physically, financially and emotionally. If I couldn't cope, how on earth could they? We didn't have much, so every waking hour was devoted to taking care of them and keeping us financially afloat. Nights when, exhausted from it all, I should have flopped into bed and fallen straight asleep were spent staring at the ceiling wondering how we would all survive, in constant fear of what would happen if I died. There was no chance of a social life or meeting anyone else. And so, like many single parents, I became increasingly lonely. I longed for Dennis to walk through the door, hold me and help me. I longed to have that love again and worried that I might never find it.

Because of what happened to me I can relate to anyone who loses his or her soulmate. Those first few nights lying alone in your bed can be terrifying. The moment you wake up in the morning and reach out for your soulmate only to find the other side of the bed cold can be the saddest moment that can happen to you. You ache to be touched, to have someone to kiss you. You long to have someone to talk to late at night, you miss those early morning conversations. When something goes wrong, who do you turn to? When something troubles you, who do you confide in? Mealtimes on your own become bleak affairs, weekends long and dreary. A walk in the park, a trip to the supermarket can make you aware of how on your own you are. Even a trip to the cinema seems lonely. Everyone but you seems to be in a couple. You pine for the days when you and your soulmate did things together. There is no one to make you feel special, no one to tell you that they love you in that special way.

LIFE WITHOUT YOUR SOULMATE

When your soulmate passes away before you, it can be difficult to adjust. You have spent so much time as a pair, doing things together, living as one, that it can be very difficult to accept that you are now on your own. Losing your soulmate can be like losing part of yourself. So many people write to me and say that without their soulmate they feel like half a person, or that they are leading half a life. Losing your soulmate can make you feel very alone, perhaps more so than with other kinds of bereavement. Suddenly your future can seem very bleak. With the death of one person you have lost your sense of security and safety, your companion, your best friend and your lover. You may think that you will never enjoy romantic love again, that you might never have another sexual relationship, you may doubt that anyone will ever love you again.

Some people tell me that they feel terribly isolated by the death of their soulmate, others tell me that they feel angry at being abandoned by them, others say that they suffer from panic attacks and simply cannot imagine a life without their love. Such is the pain of losing a soulmate that many people feel it physically. It is as though they have been hit in the middle by a heavy blow, and they behave like wounded animals. They feel that their heart is broken, quite literally. One woman who lost her husband of nineteen years wrote to me and said that had she known how painful his death was going to be for her then she would have liked to die as well.

There is an old adage that says it is better to have loved and lost than never to have loved at all. Tell this to a person who has just lost their soulmate and it will sound like the most awful cliché. But I really believe this is true. (My Romany grandmother had her own way of putting it: 'Better to have four years of happiness in a hut than forty years of drudgery in a mansion,' which is an expression I love.) Remember that the pain of losing your soulmate is as intense as the love you had for them. And the love you had for your soulmate comes from deep within your being, right inside your core. Such is the intensity of pain that you feel you will never be capable of mending your heart so that it can love again.

Your pain might be deep and heart-wrenching, but what you must keep reminding yourself, as hard as it is, is how lucky you were to have had that time, even if it was very brief, with the person you loved. When you learn to look at your loss like this, to celebrate what you were so lucky to have had rather than mourn what you have lost, you will begin to heal. I have said that we all have a soulmate, but not all of us are lucky enough to find it in this world. I count myself lucky to have shared my loved with Dennis. It may have been brief, but it gave me joy at the time, four wonderful children and a lifetime of happy thoughts and cherished memories. Part of learning to live without your soulmate is about learning to give thanks for what you had.

Whether we are spiritual or not, whether or not we believe in an afterlife, we make our soulmates immortal in our own way. We pore over letters or photographs, play their favourite music, sleep in their clothes, make regular trips to their graveside. I am all for this. It is important, as I have said earlier, to keep anyone you have loved and lost alive by talking about them when you need and want to. You should never try to pretend someone didn't exist. Not talking about them won't ease the pain of your separation. If anything, bottling it up will make it worse for you. Your soulmate, the love of your life, did exist, still does, albeit in another form, and you should talk about them and celebrate their lives as much as you need to.

The problem is that when your soulmate dies, the love you have for them doesn't. If anything, in the ensuing months and years it becomes even more intense. This can be because when our soulmate leaves us we tend to idealize them and the love that we had. Absent from the context of our daily lives, we eulogize what they were. We forget about the rows, the disagreements, the tough times. We remember only the good things – which is, of course, natural. However, it can create problems in coming to terms with the fact that our soulmate has gone and can make it difficult for us to move on and forge new relationships.

Some people are so affected by their loss they wish they were dead. They want their soulmate to come and fetch them and end their lives because they feel that they are unable to live without their love. They want to be reunited with their soulmate in spirit and live with them for eternity. You must realize that if your soulmate could come to you they would, but because your life is destined to continue they have to wait until your time has come. When that moment arrives they will be there for you. Destiny does not lie in their hands and it shouldn't lie in yours. You must learn to live out your life in the fullest way possible, and your soulmate will try and make things as easy for you as possible. Try to remember that you are put on this earth for a reason, and that you have been kept here for a reason, whether it is to look after your children, to care for others or to do something important.

Remember that you waited to find them in this life, and you can wait to meet them again in the next – and then you will have each other for eternity. Don't see the death of your soulmate as the end of your affair, see it as a brief separation, for in the greater scheme of things that is all it is. There are those who can die from a broken heart. My maternal grandmother did. But I find this tends to happen to older folk, people whose time is coming anyway and who lose the will to live and give up fighting.

LEARING TO LOVE AGAIN

We have only one *true* soulmate but that doesn't mean that we do not love more than once in our lifetime or that you cannot have a loving relationship with another person once your soulmate has passed away. It is possible to fall in love with other people and to have wonderful, loving relationships. A problem a lot of people have when they lose their soulmate is believing that being true to them means never loving again. They think that entering into a romantic relationship with another person is in effect a betrayal, or that a sexual relationship with another person might be viewed by their soulmate as an infidelity.

Losing your soulmate is very hard and can make you very lonely. Your soulmate would hate to think of you in this position. They would hate to see you so vulnerable and lonely. They wouldn't want you to be spending every night in on your own, missing them. They would want you to have a life and to share it with someone else if you wanted that. There isn't any jealousy in spirit and your soulmate knows that ultimately you belong to each other. They know that even if you were to have a serious relationship, even if you were to remarry, you two will be reunited in the spirit world. So they wouldn't just be happy if you loved again. Believe me, soulmates encourage it! Your soulmate in spirit will very often bring someone into your life with whom you can have another relationship. They can be quite conspiratorial when it comes to this, acting as matchmakers. One minute you are on your own, all miserable and lonely, and the next minute you meet someone who turns your life around. They might be a friend you have never thought about in a romantic way before, they might be a complete stranger you have met in weird circumstances, it doesn't matter who. The point is that they have been sent to you by your soulmate.

These are the people I like to call companion soulmates.

They are the ones who bring you love, comfort and happiness. They don't replace your soulmate – no one could – but they come to you so that you can love again. You might ask why your soulmate would do this for you. Well, the fact is that your soulmate loves you and they don't want you to be unhappy. They don't want to see you eating alone every night, or going on holiday on your own. They want you to have someone to share your problems, your worries and your life with. They want you to enjoy life until the moment you are reunited. And the reason why we get on so well with our companion soulmates is that they have been hand-picked for us by the person who knows us best.

I would be the first to encourage anyone who has lost someone close to them to love again and realize that this is possible. I have been lucky enough to have two wonderful men in my life, Dennis and my partner Mo, who I am blessed to have met. And I would recommend to anyone who has lost their soulmate that they should open their hearts, not lock them away, and learn to love again.

COMMUNICATING WITH YOUR SOULMATE

The bond between soulmates is so intense that I can usually ascertain within seconds of starting the reading whether this person is your soulmate. As the spirit comes through and starts communicating with me I am at once struck by an immense feeling of love. Readings with soulmates are very moving. The voice of the soulmate who has passed over is always incredibly

strong and clear in my head. Transfigurations come quite easily
and I find that I can always get a very clear vision of the person
I am communicating with in my mind. The reason for this is
simple. Spirits come to us with love. The deeper the love between
the people I read for the stronger the reading will be (which is also
why readings between parents and children work so well).

Another interesting thing is that the soulmate who has
passed over will come through almost immediately. I won't have
to ask the spirit to come through and I rarely have to ask my
spirit guide to intervene to help me out. This is because your
soulmate is waiting to talk to you, in much the same way a lover
sits by the phone waiting for a call. The likelihood is that your
soulmate has been with you throughout the day anyway, so they
know your movements and know when you are ready to talk.
And if another spirit, such as a parent or another relative, comes
through first during a reading, you can guarantee that they won't
be allowed to sit around for long! It is as though your soulmate
has grabbed the phone from them excitedly, desperate to talk to
their love.

This is why I can tell almost at once whether the people I am
reading for are soulmates. (You will notice that I always refer to
people who are soulmates in the present tense. I will say to
someone I am reading for, 'You *are* soulmates', not 'You *were*
soulmates', for just because one of you has passed over it doesn't
mean that you stop being soulmates. You only have one soulmate and you have them for eternity.)

You don't have to visit a medium to be able to communicate
with your soulmate. If you talk out loud to them or even, for that
matter, in your head they will come to you and listen to you. Just

thinking about your soulmate will bring them to you, so if ever you feel lonely or scared or just need them to be with you, think of them and they will come. Of course most of us can't actually hear what our soulmates are saying back to us. Unfortunately, not all of us are blessed with the gift of clairaudience, but that doesn't mean that the spirits of the ones we love don't try and communicate with us. Spirits, whether they have been our soulmates or not, like to visit us and at certain times they like us to know that they are there for us. As I explained in Chapter One, they can do this in simple ways, by gently blowing on our faces and bodies, by communicating via nature (when we see a butterfly or a bird, for example), or through noises. It isn't unheard of for a spirit to try and show themselves. You may suddenly notice an intense feeling of warmth around you, as though someone has suddenly turned the heating up high. You may feel a strong breeze that has seemingly come from nowhere, since all the windows are shut and the doors are closed. You may feel slightly light-headed or dizzy. These are all instances when the spirit of your soulmate could be trying to show themselves to you. You will know when this happens because these incidents will be accompanied by a great surge of love and will usually follow a period when you have been quite down, sad, ill or worried about something. The reason why this happens is that the spirit of your soulmate is desperately trying to show you that they are there for you. They want you to know that they are there for you even though you cannot see or hear them.

Soulmates in spirit tend to communicate with their loved ones down here quite frequently and this communication is always quite strong or vivid. These experiences can be very intense because of the strength of love you share. The greater the love you have had, the stronger the spiritual link.

Anna's story

In October of 2001 I had a call from Natasha Garnett, a journalist friend of mine who lives and works in London. I had met Natasha back in 1995 when she came to interview me for an article she was writing about psychics for *Vogue*. She had meant the article to be an attack on psychics and mediums and it would be something of an understatement to say that she was cynical about what I do. She had interviewed and had had readings from about thirty people who all claimed to have a 'gift', but she was unimpressed. On the night she called me to arrange a time when she could interview me, I gave her a reading on the telephone. She was so shocked and impressed by the information I gave her that she totally rewrote her article, and her opinion of mediums changed for ever. Since that night we have kept in contact, and over the years she and I have become very good friends.

When Natasha called me in October I hadn't spoken to her for a couple of months as she had been abroad a lot for work. 'You're going away again soon, aren't you?' I asked. 'To Africa,' I said. She laughed and said she was. She said she had been given a dream assignment and had been commissioned to go to Africa for a magazine and interview an artist. She said she was looking forward to the trip, not only because it meant a week's stay in Kenya, but also because by complete chance the artist she had been asked to profile was a very good friend of hers.

Immediately I told her to be careful. I had a bad feeling about the trip, I'm not sure why. Natasha travels a lot, but I had never had this feeling before. I was sure that she would be safe, but I was still uncomfortable about something. She must have thought I was fussing – as she knows all too well, I am not one for foreign travel as I hate flying – and she told me that she would be OK, the flight wasn't that long, and everything would be fine. Sadly, it wasn't to turn out like that.

Two days before Natasha was due to fly out to Kenya she received a call late at night from a friend with some bad news. Her friend, the artist Tonio Trzebinski, had been killed. 'How?' she asked, stunned. 'He was shot dead,' was the reply.

Having tucked his two young children into bed on the night of 16 October, Tonio had driven towards Karen, a wealthy suburb of Nairobi, but had never reached his destination. On a narrow dirt track off the main road Tonio was shot in the chest by a bullet fired from a 9 mm revolver. It was 9.11 p.m. According to pathology reports, the bullet, which entered his body from the right side of his chest, grazed his lung, passed through his heart and lodged itself on the left side of his chest. By the time the security guards and police reached the scene of the crime just four minutes later it was too late. Tonio Trzebinski was dead.

Kenya is a dangerous country: there are on average seventy incidences of violent crime reported each week. The crimes range from robberies to car jackings and shootings. White Kenyans are especially vigilant when it comes to protecting themselves and their properties, employing private security guards to watch over their homes and taking care not to make unnecessary car journeys at night. When Natasha heard the news, she, like many others, assumed that Tonio had fallen victim to a random act of violence. But in the days that followed a more sinister picture began to emerge – that Tonio wasn't the victim of a robbery but of a premeditated murder. The fact that nothing seemed to have been taken seemed to back up this theory; £180's worth of Kenyan shillings were found on his body. If this had been a robbery, why hadn't they taken anything?

As the facts began to emerge, so too did the theories and gossip. Some said Tonio had been killed because of his 'massive debts', some said he had made many enemies, there was even talk that he had been 'taken out by a drugs baron'. But the most salacious story of all was the story that Tonio had been at the centre of a love triangle, that Anna Trzebinski, his wife and the mother of his two children Stas and Lana, had left him and gone to America following 'weeks of arguments' over his alleged 'affair' with a 'former model', a woman called Natasha Illumberg. As these rumours spread, the world's media, from the *Daily Telegraph* to *Vanity Fair*, descended on the small suburb of Karen desperate to get a piece of a story. The *Daily Mail* branded the case as the new 'White Mischief' because of the similarity between this story and the murder of Lord Erroll in 1941.

The family couldn't, understandably, cope with this press intrusion or with all the lies they saw printed about what had happened, so they asked Natasha to come to Kenya as planned to write an article about what really went on that terrible night and set the record straight once and for all.

Of course I knew none of this at the time. I am not a great reader – I barely make it through my letters each day, I don't read the papers and the only publication I look at is *Bella* magazine. When it comes to current affairs I sometimes catch the end of the television news, but they had not covered this story.

I didn't hear from Natasha for a while. Her trip to Kenya was extended and when she returned to England she was busy writing up the story. When she did call in January I forgot to ask her how the trip had gone and knew nothing of what had happened. In fact she didn't give me much opportunity. 'Look, I hate to ask you this as I know you are very booked up,' she said, 'but could you read for a friend of mine? It's very important and she needs some help and answers.' I knew from Natasha's voice that it was urgent and so I agreed. 'She is called Anna, and she has just lost her husband.' Natasha didn't tell me anything else. She knows how I like to work – that I don't like too much information. It tends to confuse me. If I am going to read for someone I like to know as little as possible so that I concentrate 100 per cent on what I am doing. Any facts I have just tend to muddle me.

A couple of weeks later I made a call to Anna, who was staying with a friend in London. She continues the story from here:

On 16 October 2001 the sun in my universe went out. Tonio was and is my soulmate, I have always felt that. We had an incredibly intense relationship. It was often difficult, but it was based on the most powerful love and passion. I have learned that soulmates are not necessarily the ones that we have plain sailing with, but that they are the ones who agree to take on the role of making us grow: we did this for each other. Tonio took me again and again to the places where I had not only to face myself but also to overcome myself in order to grow. Our relationship was such a blessing.

Following his tragic and senseless murder I had been feeling helpless and scared. The pain was often too much to bear. We all have that useful defence mechanism called shock, but even so I felt and still feel so lost without him. I charged ahead totally driven, I carried on but was always somehow trying to escape my reality.

My friend Natasha Garnett came to Kenya right after the murder to write our story. I met her at the coast at a place called Lamu. I needed to escape my house in Karen which was being besieged by journalists and also held too many raw memories. Lamu had always been very special to Tonio and me – we had some of the happiest moments of our lives there and I thought it would be a good place to take the children. Natasha and I spent a lot of time talking, sometimes for the purpose of the article she was writing, at other times just as friends, and it was during the course of one of these conversations that she told me about Rita and her Romany background and beliefs. We had been talking about Tonio and I being soulmates, and she told me what Rita believed and about the book she had written on the subject.

Like Tonio, I had always been very spiritual and believed that there was a life after this. I had wanted to talk to someone about him but hadn't known where to go. Rita was booked up months in advance, but I knew I needed to see her. I asked Natasha whether it would be possible for me to talk to her, and she said she would do her best. Eventually an appointment was made for a telephone reading.

I was pleased but I had misgivings, as it seems more difficult to communicate with recently departed souls, and also Rita had told Natasha that she felt that the reading should be done from our home, Tonio's home, as the energy would be highest there. But nothing worked out as planned. I was travelling a great deal at the time for work so eventually we arranged for the reading to take place at a friend's flat in London as I was travelling through there on my way back from the States.

When the telephone rang I was filled with fear and antici-pation. In fact I was terrified. In a way I felt like a bride does on her wedding day, walking down the aisle to meet her husband and knowing that the two of them are going to see each other in a completely new way. I knew that I was about to communicate with Tonio – there was no doubt in my mind about that – but I hadn't envisaged what it was going to be like. I hadn't foreseen how intimate the conversation would be.

I had the presence of mind to take a notebook and pen with me. I wanted to have a record and have the option to tell the children. Through my tears I somehow managed to write my notes. She began the reading by saying that the less she knew about me the better, and then she started chatting very softly and casually, musing as she sucked on a sweet. She told me that she had been widowed in her thirties too, and that she had had to bring up her daughters on her own. And then she said, 'You've lost your soulmate.'

And then, after a short pause, she said, 'I've got him.' She told me that he was born in Africa and had been murdered there and that he was an artist. And then he came through and at once I knew it was him because, in true Tonio style, he began by ticking me off!

'You're wrong, I wasn't having an affair,' he said. When Rita

spoke to me she did so like a transmitter, speaking in the first person. 'I would never have been disloyal.' When I heard this I knew it was him. Loyalty was the most important thing to Tonio. He would never use the word 'betrayal' or 'unfaithful'. Loyalty was everything to him. He said that nothing had been 'going on with the woman' and that he 'could never love anyone the way he loved [me]'. He went on to tell me how much he loved me and repeated this throughout the reading as though he were stressing it.

Rita told me that Tonio was 'painting' a picture for her of our life. She described our house with its veranda and told me that this was where Tonio liked to be. This was true – whenever Tonio wanted to go and think he would sit on the sofa on the balcony and every evening he would watch the sun go down from there. I couldn't believe it. She said he was by the ocean fishing. After painting, fishing was Tonio's obsession and she said that he had our dog with him. Eight weeks after Tonio my beautiful Staffy Rocky had died.

She said he was laughing and he was happy and that he sent the children hugs and kisses. He said that he loved his funeral (we had held a very special service for him on the top of the hill overlooking the Rift Valley, one of his favourite places). He said that he didn't want me to call him 'dead' but to know that he is always with me and that he can hear me when I talk to him.

Then, all of a sudden, she began talking about the night he died. She spoke quickly without pausing. She said there were some men in a car following him. They pushed his car off the road. There were two to three men. They wanted his car, she said, 'It's a robbery.' Rita said all this as though she were reading an eye test card. It was as though she was just following what to say, not having any connection with the words that were coming out of her mouth. She said they took his watch, which was correct, but what astounded me was that she then went on to say that they had taken his shoes as well. Now this detail hadn't been reported in the papers and only two people knew this. I had assumed at the time that they had been stolen at the mortuary.

Then Rita went back into the first person, back into Tonio's voice. 'It was awful,' he was saying. 'I felt so scared and afraid. I gave them what they asked for. I never expected this. They have the right men,' he said, referring to the police. (In a subsequent reading Rita correctly told me that the men had been released and that Tonio was furious.) He was saying that they took his watch but wanted his car. He said that they had taken his mobile, which was also true, and that attached to the rear-view mirror of their car was a red ribbon. He shouldn't have stopped but he had no choice, the big 4 × 4 behind him was pushing him off the road, he had to stop. 'Anna,' he said, 'I should have kept going.'

Then the subject changed. He was telling Rita that he had two children; she said to me they were 'almost twins'. Well, Stas and Lana are 'Irish twins', children born within the same year. She said they were at home now and that he took care of them every day. She said that Stas loved fishing and that Lana was very creative and a great artist. Then she said to me, laughing, 'Gosh, he has the most gorgeous smile, he could charm the ducks off the pond, he could.' She also went on about his amazing voice. Tonio was known for his loud, booming, deep voice.

In the reading Rita came out with things that were so personal, things that only Tonio and I knew about. She said, for example, that I was building a holiday home. I had just bought a plot of land on the coast and hadn't told anyone about it yet. She said that he thought it was a good idea. She told me about a chair I had given Tonio for his fortieth birthday and that he was laughing about this huge chandelier I had just bought for the sitting room. He was saying I wouldn't be able to hang it from the ceiling, which again was true. He said that he wanted me to buy an eternity ring and that he was coming to me with an 'armful of roses'. Tonio would always bring me roses, never just a bunch but always an 'armful', and each time he would select a colour for how he felt. Rita said to me 'the roses are yellow, for love'.

He said he wanted me to keep feeding the birds. Our house is situated in a bird sanctuary and she told me how he loved to walk round the garden and look at all the trees. Tonio loved to do this; he would take the children with him and tell them all the names of the trees in the garden.

He talked about my work as a designer and said that he was very proud of me. He told Rita I had been making trips to America for my work and he was very excited by this. He gave me career advice, which is typical of him! Even Rita said at one point, 'God, he's bossy.' Rita had described our sitting room as being covered in boxes of materials. I am a clothes designer and so there are always boxes of things to be sent off and materials around. Usually they are in my work room, but at the time of the reading they had been moved to the sitting room. Tonio was telling Rita he wanted me to move my work into his studio, which was something I had been contemplating and have now done.

She kept telling me how much he loved me but said that he would be sending me someone in the future to be with. He wanted me to love again but the time wasn't right yet. But he stressed that I would be his in the spirit world and for eternity, which I thought *was quite funny, as he had always been extremely possessive of me!*

Rita said that Tonio had fitted two lifetimes into one, which is something that we all used to say about him because he lived life to the full. She said that at the time of his death he had been drinking too much, which was true, but she told me that he was telling her that he wouldn't have left me and that he kept wanting me to know how much he loved me. She said that he visited me the whole time, that he watched over the children and was there when we went to sleep, and that the breeze I felt from time to time was him breathing on me.

Since the reading with Rita I feel Tonio's energy everywhere. During the first months after he died I described the feeling in my diary like the moment of stillness right after a huge firework has exploded and is decorating the sky. I felt like Tonio was everywhere and that even the air was just that bit thicker because he was in it.

Before I spoke to Rita I would talk to Tonio in my head and I also wrote to him, but it wasn't like a conversation, more like a monologue. There were things that I needed to say to him because we had last seen each other under terrible circumstances, though my only feeling for Tonio as ever is and was love. I have not been angry once. That was how our relationship was. However bad things got I always loved him. Somehow our love and bond was and is separated from the details of our relationship. So I would have these things to say to him, these monologues, but since I have been talking to Rita I now realize that these aren't monologues, they really are conversations. What I liked about the reading was that at no time did Rita make me feel that the reading was about her, it was about the two of us and she acted as a transmitter. She encouraged me to talk to

Tonio whenever I wanted and said that I didn't need to do it through her. If I talked he would listen.

I miss Tonio more than should be humanly possible and I simply cannot yet imagine my loss – I am stunned. But I no longer feel so lonely, I have lost any fear of death, my belief in life and my faith in a higher power have multiplied and I feel like a much better person somehow. Most of all I feel totally protected and I really feel that he is looking after the three of us. Rita has helped my pain and got me through rough patches. She is so very lucky to have this gift and we are so blessed that she uses it to help people like Tonio and me. I love my husband more than ever, and in a strange kind of way the rest of my life is a formality now that I must complete alone, and I need to learn certain lessons without my knight.

There is no way that I would have committed suicide, but to be honest I felt like I was living a half-life and that I would only start breathing again when I was reunited with him. My job is to stay on and look after our children, the two angels that we brought into this world. I always knew this, but somehow the knowledge that he is here with us makes that easier. I realize now that there is a reason for my life to go on and I have to embrace that. But if it weren't for this reading I would have lost my belief in life. Rita helped me believe in life again. And she made me feel very safe, because she had told me and proved to me that he was around us. Since this first reading I have received endless practical advice and direction as well as the most loving messages from him via Rita. I know I am not alone and that someday I will be with him again for eternity, which is a very beautiful thought. Rita's gift has restored light in my life, my sun is in my universe; I cannot see it, but I do feel its warmth.

I have said that the love between soulmates conquers everything and this really is shown here. Anna and Tonio had been through a difficult time in their marriage and when they had last seen each other it had not been on good terms. That must have made Tonio's death more difficult to cope with, but as this reading shows Tonio came with nothing but love for Anna, all was forgotten and he made a point of telling her throughout the reading how much he loved her. One of the reasons why he came through so clearly and quickly was because he needed her to know this more than anything.

I have spoken to Anna a couple of times since that first reading and every time Tonio comes through so strongly and with so much love for her. In a recent conversation something very odd happened. Anna called me from her house in Kenya and said she had been away for a few weeks. I sensed she had been walking and she told me that this was true. She said over the past few weeks walking in the bush had given her the space and the time to think, and that when she was at one with nature she felt closer to Tonio than ever. She said she hadn't been walking alone but had gone with a Samburu warrior who was acting as her guide. While we were speaking I said to her quite out of the blue, 'Tonio has just walked into the room.' I didn't expect her to say anything because of course she couldn't see him. We carried on chatting about this and that when I said to her, 'He is touching your toes.' Anna gasped, but said nothing and we continued to talk. Then I interrupted the conversation once again, 'He doesn't like your hair braided, he wants to undo it for you.' Anna couldn't believe what I was telling her. She said when I had told her that Tonio had entered her sitting room her

Samburu guide had just walked in, he then touched her foot. Whilst she was on the telephone to me he took her hair and started to unbraid it for her which was totally out of character to be so familiar. I am sure that this was Tonio and the reason I was convinced of this was because he was telling me so.

It seems that Tonio is able to move his spirit into the body of the Samburu warrior, he hasn't taken possession of him, because it seems that Anna's guide is still very much his own person. But what I think is happening here is that Tonio is transferring his energies to the warrior so that he is able to help Anna and heal her. I have to say this is incredibly rare and I haven't come across it many times before, but what it shows us is that, as I say time and time again, the love between soulmates is so intense that it seems to transcend everything and knows no barriers.

9. Coping with Suicide

The death of anyone close to us causes an enormous amount of pain and hurt, but when someone we love very much takes their own life, our feelings of grief, our sadness and our sense of loss are further complicated by other emotions such as guilt, failure, shame and anger. Some people who lose a loved one to suicide experience a great sense of abandonment and betrayal too.

We are taught to frown upon suicide. Most religions do not approve of it, and culturally we are led to believe that it is a coward's way out. We are taught that whatever life throws at us we should just get on with it and make the best of it. I don't agree with this. In my opinion it is a very brave person who takes his or her own life. Wanting to put an end to your life is extreme, and I think that we must learn to accept that in certain situations some people really just cannot cope with their lot. These are people who are suffering in a way that we cannot begin to imagine, people who are so depressed they have not only lost all sense of hope and a future but cannot even cope with the present. They are people who are so full of despair they no longer feel they can ask for help, and believe that even if they did it wouldn't do any good. They feel cut off from the rest of us. They feel isolated in their pain, they feel rejected, or that they have failed. They have no self-esteem, no confidence. They can no longer communicate with the people around them. They are lost souls. They feel like they are a burden to the rest of us. And so they want to put an end to all those feelings and to be at peace at last.

Whilst I do think that these people are brave, suicide is not something I would recommend to anyone who is going through a bad time. However bad things seem in life there is always a route we can take that will make things better. The problem is that people who are very low and depressed often can't see the wood for the trees. They are usually so confused and their mind is in such a fog that they can't rationalize a way out of their problem. Moreover, these feelings of despair and depression are usually accompanied by other states of mind such as low self-esteem. Even if an alternative path is offered to them they might feel they are not up to it. They may be worried that they will fail again or let everyone down.

I get many letters from people who are in this state of mind and thanks to the readings I give them I am usually able to find a way of giving them faith in themselves and in their future. I am able to do this because their spirit guides help me find ways of talking them out of it. They might tell me about a project that the person has always been interested in but has never pursued, and they may say that the time is now right to do something about it. They might talk to me about a potential friend that person is going to meet or about a soulmate that is waiting for them round the corner. What these people need is a belief in their own life: they need to feel that their life is worth living, and hopefully my readings can give them that. But there are other ways to help someone who is feeling suicidal, including yourself if you are feeling that way, without having to visit a medium. When I can't read for someone who is in this position I always write to them and give them the following advice.

Advice for those with suicidal thoughts

1. If you are unable to talk to those close to you, you must seek counsel from someone else. We all need someone to talk to, we all need advice, but sometimes the people closest aren't actually the right person for that job. They may know too much about us, they see us in a certain way. If we are feeling very broken then talking to a stranger can be very refreshing because they will approach us in a different and new light. They might see things in us that no one else can see. They might be able to tell us where we have been going wrong and guide us back onto the right path. Throughout the UK and Ireland there are many hundreds of organizations that offer this kind of help and a lot of it is free. You don't have to see a therapist, you could go to a self-help group, you could call the Samaritans, or even see your local priest. All these people are there for you and are willing to help you through your bad time.

2. Draw strength and courage from the spirit world. You may feel that you have had a bad time and may not be able to cope with what life has thrown at you, but have faith. Pray to God, pray to your spirit guides for help and guidance, and whilst you do this take time to think of what is actually good about your life. Make a list of the things that you like about yourself and your life and the people you know. And understand that whilst the major events of our lives are fated, you can make a difference to what happens to you – you *can* come through a bad patch, you *can* make things better. I think our lives have become so materialistic these days that we sometimes fail to see the good around us. We are so worried about money and success that we don't see what we have actually been given. Having spiritual beliefs, whatever they are, can help you through the bad times. They can give you hope and faith and help you to appreciate the life you have.

3. Read my books. I don't say this out of vanity or self-promotion, I say this because the books are uplifting and are full of hope. I read for a man last year who was on the brink of suicide. The night he planned to take his life he had been to his sister's and she had lent him one of my books. He wasn't going to read it, it wasn't really 'his thing', but something inside him drew him to read it that evening. He was halfway through the book when he realized he no longer wanted to take his life. He wrote to me afterwards and said he had been so moved by stories of other people's bravery and courage in times of real adversity that it had given him the strength to make something of his life. Sometimes, looking at other people's lives, seeing how much they have suffered and seeing how they have coped, can give us a great deal of inner strength and the courage to face our own life.

Another reason why I do not recommend suicide as a 'way out' for people who are very down and depressed is that I don't think they have any idea how much it will affect those around them after they have gone. The problem with the act of suicide is that it always causes much more suffering than it heals. The loved ones who are left behind are forced to go through so much pain and so many questions. Not only do they mourn the death, they punish themselves with the thought that they could and should have done something to prevent the suicide. They feel that they have failed, they feel guilty, and some people never really recover from that.

Guilt is the primary emotion that people go through when they lose a loved one to suicide, and I'm afraid it is unrelenting. They just cannot accept that this death was beyond their control, and they torture themselves with this. Had someone died in another way, been a victim of a fatal accident, died from an illness, or were even, God forbid, murdered, then there would be someone else to blame. But with a suicide, people don't really have this outlet for their anger, and rather than blaming the person who took their own life they tend to turn on themselves.

I read for a great many people who have lost loved ones in this way, and it doesn't surprise me that they come to me. Often these relatives and friends are so deeply troubled by their loss that they just don't know how to cope with it all. They want to know why they feel angry and bitter, or hurt and betrayed. They come to me to find out whether it has been their fault, whether they were to blame, but most of all they want to know why. Why did this person feel so lost that they had to end their life?

Those left behind are just as much a victim of suicide as the ones who take their own life.

A CRY FOR HELP

Although a great many people *try* to take their own life, very few people actually intend to go through with it. Rather, these people are making a serious cry for help. Unable to express their sense of despair or to communicate their fears to their loved ones, they try to get our attention in this way. Sadly, all too often this goes wrong and they are not reached in time. Of course the great irony of this is that rather than being 'helped' their life ends up being cut short. These are what I call 'accidental deaths'.

Whether the death has occurred accidentally or intentionally, I find that when I read for people in these situations the spirit will come through extremely quickly and clearly. Once that person reaches the spirit world they will be very aware of the pain and the hurt that their death has caused and they will want to come and make amends for it. They will want to say sorry for having created so much trouble. If the death was intentional they will want you to know that they are without pain and are now at peace and that there was nothing that you could have done to prevent it. If, on the other hand, the death was accidental, then this will be stressed over and over again. They will tell me the circumstances in which they died to prove to you that it is them talking; they will be very specific about where and when it happened and the events leading up to the death. To prove that it was not intentional.

Angela's story

Because spirits visit us they know what we go through when they die. They see our grief and hurt, they see the tears we weep for them, the hole that their death creates in our lives. This is why spirits are so quick to come to someone like me – because they are desperate for their families to know that they are all right. In cases where the person who has passed over either has taken their own life, or is believed to have done so, I find that the spirit will be even more determined to get to me. These spirits will go to extraordinary lengths to get their message across to their loved ones as this next story shows.

This story began when I was interviewed for an Irish radio station called Radio Highland in early 2002, and it is told by Angela, who lives in County Donegal, Ireland.

Our worst nightmare began on the evening of 9 November 2001. I had come back from hospital with a friend of mine after they had had a check-up. We were having a cup of tea before I returned home when my daughter Eileen knocked at the door. I could see the police officers behind her. I will never forget her words to me, they will haunt me until the day I die: 'Mum,' she said, 'you have to be strong. They have found Padraig dead.' I just started screaming, 'It can't be true, it can't. I must be dreaming!' I collapsed to the floor.

I had spoken to my lovely son in the USA just a couple of days before. He had been living in Colorado. We had talked about our plans to meet in Chicago in two weeks' time to celebrate his and his sister's birthdays on 23 and 24 November. They would have been twenty-two and twenty-three years old. We were all very excited about the trip, as we hadn't seen Padraig for a year and a half. He had gone to the States to work for a youth scheme. My husband Gerard had sadly passed from cancer in 1997 so my children really were my life.

After many calls to the States we eventually got hold of the coroner, who told us that Padraig was found hanging by a belt at the back of a Wal-Mart store and that the car he had borrowed to go to a U2 concert in Denver was forty miles from where his body was found. On examination the car was found to have a flat tyre and the spare also had a flat. How on earth was he able to drive that forty miles? Had he been murdered, we wondered? It was just all so mysterious. After getting his body back here to be buried beside his father, my daughter and I went to Colorado to see what had happened and to see what we could find out. We didn't get much satisfaction. We had no answers. My sister Breda who lives in Chicago with her husband and four boys joined us in Colorado for support. It was terrible because we came back to Ireland none the wiser than when we had gone out to the States.

For the next few months we tried to get on with our lives as best we could. We cried a lot and barely slept. Our lives had been turned upside down. It was a living hell.

One day I was listening to the radio and a lady on our local station was saying that she had been for a reading with Rita Rogers, the medium, and how it brought her great comfort. I had heard that the presenter of the programme was going to telephone Rita, so I rang the station and got in touch with him. He said that Rita was going to talk to him on the programme, but that she wouldn't do readings live on air. I begged him to try and help and see if she would talk to me but he wasn't that optimistic. I listened to the programme and I could hear the presenter asking if she could tune into anything during the interview. She went very quiet for a while. And then she said that she was picking up a boy who had passed very tragically. Then she mentioned my name: she said 'Angela' and that she was getting the initial 'P'. As it was over the radio she said that she wouldn't read, but she asked whoever this was to write to her. I did immediately, enclosing a photograph of Padraig. About three weeks later there was a message on my telephone telling me to get in touch with her. I rang back and an appointment was made.

I was very nervous when the reading began, but Rita's lovely soft voice put me at ease straight away. First of all she said that she had two males in spirit with her, one much younger than the other. My husband who had passed away almost five years ago then came through first, assuring us all of his love for us and how sorry he was about our son's death. Rita was able to say that he had passed over from cancer and that he had been very hard-working. Rita said that he had our son with him and that he was the kind of boy who lit the room up with his beautiful smiling face. She said that he was calling me Mom and that he had passed over very tragically. She said that he had taken his own life and that at the time he did this he was coming up to his twenty-third birthday. She said the tragedy had happened in the USA where he was working.

He told her that he had a car and that he had gone to the U2 concert in Denver. I was amazed by the details she was giving me and just how accurate they were. He said to her that he had broken down on the way back. He said that it was a very isolated place and that he had had to walk several miles. She said that he was exhausted and very cold. She said to me that he smoked some cannabis at the concert. She described to me how he was feeling then and that he was saying that he just couldn't cope. She said to me that he was telling her that he had been having some problems with someone he worked with. Feeling lost in the middle of nowhere it was just too much for him and he suffered from some kind of brainstorm. She said that he went behind the Wal-Mart building and hanged himself. She said that he didn't know what had happened until he saw that his father had come for him.

He said over and over again during the reading how sorry he was and that although he was very happy where he was he wished he could turn the clock back. He said how much he loved my daughter and me and that he didn't know what he was doing at the time.

Padraig also said that he didn't like his sister's hair (she had recently dyed it blonde) and that I should replace my glasses with contact lenses. During the reading a good friend of mine, Rose, who had recently died of cancer, came through and said that she was devastated by Padraig's passing. (In fact her husband had already told me that.) She said that she saw my son and that she was watching out for him. And my father too came to me. Padraig was also able to relay to Rita that he had a sister in spirit called Laura. I had had a miscarriage before I had Padraig. I didn't have a name for her when I lost her but Rita seemed adamant that she was a 'Laura'. After the reading I remembered that when my husband lived in London before we were married we used to go to the cinema a lot. We had seen Dr Zhivago *a couple of times and I remember saying to him one night after a performance that if I had a little girl I would like to call her 'Lara' after the character played by Julie Christie. Of course I had forgotten about this as it had been such a long time ago, and when our first daughter was born we named her Eileen after his mother. Padraig also sent his love to several of his friends: he had so many. He had a lot of advice for his sister and said that he liked her new boyfriend Joe. There was so much in this reading, I could almost write a book on the subject.*

Rita finished the reading by saying that Padraig was well and much loved in spirit. Although the reading didn't bring Padraig back and I still miss him terribly, it means so much to me to know that he didn't suffer too much. Yes, I am heartbroken and know that

I won't recover from this. But I have drawn comfort from knowing what happened to him, that he wasn't murdered and that he is safe and well and with people he knows in spirit, people like his father who will look after him until we are all reunited. I have to say that even if I hadn't got through to Padraig in spirit, I would have been comforted just talking to Rita. She is a lovely, warm, healing person. She helped us all a great deal and for that I give so many thanks.

PEACE AT LAST

For some people life just becomes too much. Life is a gift, but not all of us can cope with the trials it puts us through. We shouldn't judge people who can't cope and need to find release in death, because for them it really is the only answer. Would you condemn a person who had a terribly painful illness for looking forward to their death because they knew they would no longer suffer? Would you say to them, stay alive at any cost because that is what God would want? Would you tell them to grin and bear it and make the most of what they have? The answer is probably not. We would mourn their death and feel sad for those around them, but ultimately we would draw some comfort from the fact that they were no longer suffering and console our own loss with the knowledge that they were now at peace. It is strange, then, that we don't feel the same about people who decide that they must take their life because they cannot cope with the mental suffering it is causing them. It is odd, and perhaps even prejudiced, that we don't give them the same compassion as those who die from other causes. Fortunately, though, attitudes to mental illness are beginning to change. As we come to understand more and more about how people suffer from mental illnesses and depression, we will begin to feel more comfortable and understanding about suicide.

I do not agree with people who argue that people who commit suicide will be punished in the afterlife or will go straight to hell. In all the years I have been reading, I have no evidence to back up either of these absurd claims. Whenever I read for someone who has taken their own life they appear to be happy, well and at peace in spirit. I once read for a poor woman who had lost her eighteen-year-old son. He had been very depressed following a break-up with his girlfriend and had taken his own life. The mother was naturally terribly distressed and was desperate to make contact with her son to find out why he had done it. She visited a medium she had found advertised in her local paper. During the 'reading' the medium told the mother that she couldn't make contact with her son because he had gone to hell. Of course the medium couldn't make contact with her son, but that wasn't because he was in hell, it was because she wasn't a medium. (The 'medium' charged the woman for this 'reading' as well!) When I heard this story I was so incensed. It enrages me when people pose as mediums in order to make money, not only because it is fraudulent but also because it can cause so much damage to other people.

Learning to live with suicide is very difficult. When someone very close to us takes their own life we have to deal with so much. On top of the grief that we would normally suffer had our loved one died of natural causes or in an accident, for example, we also have to bear the heavy burden of guilt. In all my years of reading for people who have lost loved ones to suicide I have never met anyone who did not in some way blame themselves for that death. It doesn't matter how far-fetched or irrational this is, people just cannot help feeling responsible. And often this blame manifests itself not just in a psychological form but physically too.

I once read for a mother of a schizophrenic who lost her boy to suicide. Her son, who in the past had been twice sectioned, was not getting the help he needed and, being over the age of eighteen, there was little his mother could do. Both the authorities and his doctors did little to help. He was prescribed medication, but of course he sometimes didn't want to take it. Eventually, in order to free himself from the demons in his mind, he took his life by jumping from the window of a tall building.

When his mother came to me, she must have weighed less than six stone. She cannot have been more than forty-five yet she looked ten years older and her thin hands were covered in cuts where she had dug her nails into her skin and drawn blood. As she sat there rocking back and forth, she kept saying it was her fault. She said she should have done more, but she couldn't. She said that had she been a 'good mother' then she would have cared for him herself, but that she had had to work. But during the reading her son kept saying over and over again that it had nothing to do with her, that she had been the most wonderful mother but that he could no longer live like that and be such a burden to her and a liability to himself. She knew it was him because I was able to name his different personalities. He wanted her to know that he was happy because now he was just himself and he said that no number of pills or hospitals could have given him that. She was so relieved at the end of the reading that she just couldn't stop crying.

Julie's and Anita's story

Cases like the one above show that we cannot always stop people from taking their lives no matter how much we love them or are close to them. They make the decision that they can no longer cope with this world, and no amount of persuasion can help. In cases like these I ask people to learn to accept this in the way that they would terminal cancer or a car crash. If there was nothing they could have done they must accept this and not punish themselves over the death but mourn and grieve it and celebrate what life that person had.

The next story is about Janette, a lovely young woman who on the face of it 'had it all' and so much to live for. But inside Janette could no longer cope and so, tragically, she decided to end her life. The story is told from two perspectives, first by Janette's sister, Julie, who was the last to see her alive, and then by her mother, Anita. The three of them were extremely close and Julie and Anita always come together for their readings.

Julie:

I was the last person to see Janette alive. We were all worried about her and I had telephoned to say that I would call to see her the following morning. Although I felt helpless, I wanted to reassure Janette that we were all there for her no matter what, and that all we wanted was for her to get better.

Janette was my only sister and was four years younger than me. We had always been close and were both very close to our mother as well. I found Janette's depression very hard to understand. I tried to support her and help her make decisions about her life, but she was reluctant to show her feelings and sometimes she was distant – like a stranger. She hated the word depression and tried to pretend that she was OK. But she wasn't. How I wanted the old Janette back and for things to be normal. Before her illness Janette had always been so full of life and fun and wanted to do well at everything. She was so smart and had excellent dress sense. She always seemed prettier, slimmer and more confident than me. She was beautiful.

I was a housewife bringing up my two young daughters Emma and Rachel. I had dropped Emma off at nursery in the morning and went to see Janette. Janette was quite quiet that morning and seemed anxious about Rachel who, as a toddler, was all over the place. I chatted away and played with Rachel. I thought that Janette seemed a lot better, but for some reason I didn't want to leave her. I asked her if she would like to come with me to pick Emma up, but she said that she didn't want to come, so I left her. On the way home I rang Mum to tell her that I thought Janette was improving. I didn't know then how wrong I was.

This day soon turned into the worst day of my entire life. When my stepfather called me later to say that Janette had taken her own life, I crumbled. I just could not believe it. I couldn't take it in. Why hadn't I seen the signs? We were very close, why hadn't she said something to me, talked to me? Had I said something wrong? Had I been too wrapped up in my own life? Was it my fault? Why hadn't I insisted that she come with me to pick up Emma? Could I have prevented it?

I had reassured Mum that Janette was improving and so on top of everything else that was going through my head at that moment was the thought that I had let her down as well. I rushed over to Mum's, my head spinning. We were all in shock and tried to comfort each other. Mum never once blamed me. We all felt guilty in our own way.

A local vicar came to see us and was very supportive. People from the local paper also came, but to be honest I can't remember much about the rest of that day, it was all a blur. Although it was all happening, I felt detached from reality. The sheer horror of what had happened to Janette was so, so hard to cope with. How could my beautiful younger sister die in such a tragic way? It was too much to bear.

I tried to be as much support as I could to Mum. We were absolutely shattered. Friends and family sent their sympathy cards and we gave thanks for Janette's life at her funeral, but Janette's death had created this terrible void in my life, an empty hole where my sister should be. I felt so cold and numb.

I went home after the funeral to take care of my daughters. I had to carry on for their sake. My husband Gary was very under-standing. After the girls were tucked up in bed at night I would just cry and cry. And along with the sadness and the numbness I felt I was also feeling so guilty. Why had Janette become so ill when I was lucky enough to have such a wonderful life? It just didn't seem right or fair.

With Janette's death my life didn't seem that wonderful any more. I didn't go out other than to do the school run. If I went shopping I felt as though complete strangers could see my pain. Each day it was as though I was just going through the motions — I wasn't actually living. I tried to be normal for my family's sake, but inside I was in turmoil. I was also beginning to suffer from extremely bad dreams.

In a desperate attempt to find some comfort and some meaning in Janette's death, Mum and I went to church every Sunday. We hoped it would bring us peace of mind. We would pray for Janette. I thought she was lost for ever. The feelings that go through your head at times like this can be quite irrational, but then you aren't thinking straight anyway. I remember thinking that when spring arrived it felt so wrong. How could life just carry on as normal when I was so full of grief?

A friend of Mum's gave her Rita Rogers's telephone number and an appointment was made for Mum to see her. I said that I would go with her for the reading. We did everything together when it came to Janette. I have to say that I was extremely apprehensive about the reading. I had never had my fortune told and I didn't know what to expect. But nothing could make me feel worse than I did already, so I went along with the plan.

Ash House, where Rita lived back then, was a lovely old house, full of character. When we arrived we were shown into a sitting room which was very peaceful and quiet. The large fireplace was adorned with horse brasses and there was a vase of fresh flowers on the polished coffee table. We felt very welcomed. Rita came into the room and introduced herself and led us into her reading room. This room was very light and nicely decorated in pink with a huge bay window. Rita was extremely friendly and warm, but with her black hair and dark eyes she looked quite striking. She chatted generally for a while and I began to relax. Then she asked if anyone in the last five years had passed over. We nodded.

Rita began to tell us that Mum had lost a daughter and that I had lost my sister. She said that Janette had been very ill and told us exactly how she had died. We both sobbed. She gave some more details to do with Janette's personal life, things that no one else could have known. I could hardly believe my ears. Rita could actually hear Janette and passed messages on to us.

Through Rita, Janette said that she hadn't wanted to hurt us but that she was unable to carry on the way she was. She had been in such a state before she died and she felt that she had no other way out. She hated being ill. She said she was very sorry and wanted us to know she loved us very much and that there was nothing we could have done. I was so relieved to know that Janette was safe and not lost for ever. I could imagine her in a much better place and not somewhere in my dark dreams. I understood that none of this was my fault and that no one else was to blame. Janette went on to say that she didn't want us to be sad for her.

When we left Rita's I felt so much lighter, so much stronger and I felt ready to carry on. We have seen Rita on many occasions. Each time Janette comes through and brings other friends and relatives who have passed over. Janette, through Rita, tells us about what is going on in our lives today and there are many times when we all just have a good laugh.

I now know that Janette wants us to be happy, and although I will always miss her I know that one day we will be together again.

Anita:

In the autumn of 1989 I lost my darling daughter Janette. She was only twenty-six years old and had always been the most wonderful *daughter and sister to my other daughter, Julie, who was nearly four years older than her.*

Janette had been ill with depression for a couple of years. We didn't realize how ill she was or, for that matter, why. She had a very good job in a local bank and had been married for years and on the face of it seemed to have a lot going for her. But Janette was a perfectionist and there seemed to be something she was unable to do. The problem was that because Janette was an adult and was married, there was little I could do when it came to talking to the doctors. The information had to come from her, but she was unable to explain to anyone what the cause of her illness was. Indeed she didn't want anyone to know she was ill and wouldn't have the word depression mentioned. Eventually, things got so bad that Janette and her husband separated. Janette moved back home, and we all thought she was getting better when she bought her own house.

The day she died she seemed a lot better. I had spoken to her on the phone that day and Julie had visited her with her youngest daughter. I was in the supermarket buying pork chops for her supper when I received a message to go home. I knew instinctively that it was about Janette and also that she was dead. I can't tell you how I felt. You would have to experience something like that yourself to understand what I was going through. I wouldn't want anyone else to go through that, but of course I know that, sadly, people have done and will do in the future.

The weeks after Janette's death were a complete blur for me. Friends were wonderful, they shopped and brought food into the house. My family meanwhile just clung together in despair. Janette had been separated from her husband at the time of her death and she had a boyfriend, but in the midst of this sadness there was no animosity, instead the two were united in their grief. I honestly can't say much more about it, words can't describe what I went through. The feeling of 'if only' was at the forefront of every thought I had. But it was the realization that there was nothing we could do, that we couldn't change anything, that we wouldn't see or hear Janette again, that was truly unbearable.

A friend of mine knew Rita Rogers. I had no idea who she was at the time, but it was arranged that Julie and I would go and visit her for a reading. Despite the fact that we shared a friend, Rita didn't know anything about Janette and her death, but I was amazed by her reading. She told me immediately that I had lost my daughter and she told us how she died and the whole story right from the beginning. Because Janette was married and I have to respect the feelings of other people involved in this story, I don't want to go into precise details – it's too personal and too painful. But what Rita did tell us, which helped me a lot, was that Janette was happy. She said that she was sorry to have upset anyone, but she could not have carried on the way she was feeling. Rita explained to us that Janette was very ill and that this was why she had taken her life. She hadn't done it for any specific reason, she had done it because she was so ill.

Julie and I have visited Rita every six months since 1989 and I can honestly say that without those readings I don't think I would have been able to carry on. The first few times Rita didn't remember who we were, which is fair enough since she does so many readings and helps so many people, so each time she recounted the story of Janette's death and the circumstances surrounding it. Now she knows who we are we don't have to go through this stage, but each time I am amazed by what Rita tells me. We have sobbed on Rita's couch so often, but at the end of it we just feel so much better.

During the readings Janette always comes to us with other relatives of ours who have passed over and she always gives us so much evidence to prove that she is still part of our lives – she says things that no one else knows about. She likes, for example, to talk about Julie's daughters, her nieces. She is always able to tell Julie what is going on in their lives, what they are up to with their ponies and so on. She even said on one occasion that one of the ponies had something wrong with its legs, which was correct. And she said that Julie's husband had something wrong with his knees and that they would have to be operated on, which again was true. It's as though Janette really is watching over Julie and her family, which means a lot to us.

Once, we went after the reading to visit a friend of mine whose daughter had just given birth to twin boys. Janette knew this and told Rita. She said that I had planned to give ten pounds to the mother as a gift for her children, which was completely right, but Janette was telling Rita to tell me that this wasn't enough, that I must give them ten pounds each. Needless to say I did what Janette told me! But it's this type of thing that really makes me laugh and puts me in no doubt that one day we will all be together again.

There are so many instances when Rita would have been unable to say what she told us without having heard it from Janette herself. Recently, for instance, Janette told Rita to tell us that she had Benji and was looking after him and that he was fine. She said that they had been delighted to be with each other again. What Rita didn't know was that Janette and I shared a Westie. He was called Benji and at the ripe old age of seventeen he had died. You can imagine how I felt when Rita mentioned Benji's name – the tears just fell. But they weren't tears of sadness.

By meeting Rita and therefore communicating with Janette, I have come to see that there is an afterlife. The evidence of life after death in these readings is overwhelming and in many ways I owe Rita my life, because in the early days, the despair and the guilt over Janette's death was too much to bear. And to know that Janette is now happy is all the comfort I need.

10. *Coping with Tragedy*

In this book I have discussed ways in which we can learn to live with the death of someone close to us, how we can come to terms with that loss and learn to live again. As I have said, some people never recover from the death of a loved one, though they can learn to accept it and adjust. But what happens to someone when they lose more than one person they love? What happens to people whose lives are repeatedly blighted by personal tragedy? How would you cope if you lost more than one person you loved very deeply in a short space of time? Could you cope? Could you recover, accept those tragedies and learn to adjust?

Over the years I have had my own share of personal tragedy. Although each has saddened me I have been able to accept these as part of the fabric of life. Thanks to my belief in the afterlife and my gift I am perhaps better equipped to cope with this sort of pain than most, but that said, there have been times during my career when I have been so taken aback by the degree of tragedy that some people have to bear that I have had to question whether I would be able to cope had I been in their shoes.

I have read for many people over the years who have suffered terrible losses – parents who have lost all their children in a house fire; grandparents who have had to cope with bringing up two little children after their son and daughter-in-law have been killed in a road accident; the young woman who lost her brother, her best friend and then her lover, all within a year.

People are actually much more resilient than we imagine them to be, and when they suffer in this way I usually find that they draw on an inner strength they did not even know they had. They learn to survive, to carry on in some way. They will walk into my reading room and sit down as if nothing has happened at all. They will seem quite together, quite positive even, and it's only when the reading begins and I start to get these names one after another that I actually realize what has happened and how much the person sitting in front of me has suffered.

Then, when I look closer, what I notice time and time again with people who have been through great tragedy is that the life has gone out of them. Yes, they are living, yes, they are coping and functioning on some level, but the 'life' has gone from their soul. You will see no joy in their eyes, no laughter in their hearts and the smile they give is empty. People who have suffered like this find it very hard to enjoy themselves again. Try as they might, they find it hard to get into the spirit of anything. They seem distant, distracted and disconnected from what is going on. They might find it hard to socialize, difficult to work, to talk, and so they keep their focus on very simple things like housework, menial tasks and chores, gardening. They like to concentrate on things that they know they can cope with. They hate surprises, they don't much care for parties or holidays or any sort of event. After all, when life has dealt them so many blows, how can they derive any happiness from it? There is no room in their hearts and souls for any emotion other than grief.

People who have been hurt in this way live very much day by day and the reason for this is simple: if you have lost many people in your life, after a point you lose all sense of hope. How can you hold on to hope when your life has been a series of tragic losses? Why plan for the future when you may not even have one? These are the questions that people in this situation ask me.

Recently I read for a woman who had lost her mother and daughter in a car accident. In order to help her through her terrible grief her husband had decided that they needed some time away together. He booked a holiday in Australia, as he knew it was somewhere she had always wanted to visit, but when he gave her the tickets she just stared at him and said, 'Why on earth would I want to do that?' The woman knew that he was only trying to help, and she admitted to me that had he brought those tickets home before the accident she would have been thrilled, but what did she want with sitting on a beach, staying in hotels and sightseeing now? 'It would have been the holiday of a lifetime,' she said, 'but I don't feel like I have a life any more, Rita.' I have said earlier that when someone close to us dies part of us goes too, so if we lose a lot of people we are very close to, then each time another part of our soul will die too. When this woman lost her mother she lost her past, her childhood, so much of her life. With her daughter, her only child, taken from her too she lost her future, her hope, her sense of promise and fulfilment. It's no wonder that she felt dead inside.

Humans can cope with only so much pain. After we reach a certain threshold we just can't take any more and we go numb. We switch on to autopilot and live like that. We withdraw into our own world and find it very hard to communicate with others. The problem for people who lose a lot of people they love is that they don't really know where to begin when it comes to the grieving process. The woman in this case lost her mother and her child simultaneously. Whilst she adored her mother, she could not mourn her to start with because she was too busy grieving for her child. It was only when she realized how much her child's death was hurting her that she really *felt* the loss of her mother, for suddenly there was no one there to support her.

I am often asked what people can do to help someone in this position and all I can say is, be there for them. You will probably never understand the sheer magnitude of the pain they feel and you won't be able to make that pain any better, but by being there you are showing the support and giving them the love they need.

As for the people who have suffered, what I would say to them is, live with the knowledge that all isn't gone. Your loved ones are still with you and visit you and love you, as I think this next story proves.

Margaret's story

For some time now I have been reading for a very dear woman called Margaret, whom I have the deepest respect and admiration for. On 4 June 1992 her life changed for ever when her two children were killed in a horrific car accident. Vicky and Steven had taken a lift with some friends and were driving not two hundred yards from the family home when their car was knocked off the road, down a slope and into a verge. All five children in the car were killed instantly. Here Margaret tells her incredibly brave and moving story of what happened and how she coped with this terrible tragedy:

My world fell apart and my life felt worthless after my two children, Vicky and Steven, died in a car crash along with three other friends. Vicky was twenty, Steven, just eight at the time of the accident. Vicky was an outgoing girl, with blonde shoulder-length hair and a petite frame. With his blonde hair and blue eyes Steven was angelic-looking, but though he may have had the face of innocence he had the wisdom of a twenty-eight-year-old. You see, I had been married twice. With my first husband I had two children, Vicky and her older brother Shaun, then later on Steven appeared. Despite the large age gap all the children were very close and so Steven was much older for his years than a normal eight-year-old. In fact, he didn't have much time for younger children, he found them annoying.

We never really got to the bottom of what had happened, what had caused the accident. I suppose I went into shock. The enormity of emotions I went through and the feelings of guilt I suffered were devastating. I couldn't make sense of anything, life was very much day by day, and I wasn't sure how I was going to cope with the loss of my children. The doctor gave me some pills, but would only allow me to have one dose a day. I think she worried that if I had any more in the house I might take an overdose.

People around me were wonderful. Vicky's friends would drop by constantly to make sure I was OK. They took me on a trip to Blackpool and the first Christmas, determined that I shouldn't spend it at home, they took me on a holiday to the Canary Islands. But still

I couldn't cope with what had happened. Realizing that I needed to get some help in order to make sense of my emotions, a friend suggested that I should go and see Rita Rogers. This friend was in fact the mother of Lisa, one of Vicky's friends who had also died in the crash. She said the reading had helped her, but I wasn't convinced.

To be completely honest I was a non-believer in mediums and clairvoyance. A woman I worked with used to go to a spiritualist church every week. 'Off to the church again?' I'd scoff. I thought she was daft for going. But one day Lisa's mother said to me that Rita had had a message for me from Vicky and Steven. 'Yeah, right-o,' I replied. But an appointment had already been made for me to see Rita and at this stage I was on autopilot, so I went along with the suggestion, if only because I did not have the strength to object.

At my first meeting with Rita I was incredibly nervous. She must have realized this because she spoke for a while about her own life, her family and her friends in order to calm me down, and this did put me at ease. As I began to relax Rita told me that she knew I was nervous and that she knew I hadn't been to a medium before. Then the reading began.

Rita told me my name and told me I had three children She then said that they were half-brother and -sister, which was true. She described Vicky and Steven to me and told me then that I had trimmed Vicky's hair for her — but laughed and said that it wasn't straight. I had done Vicky's hair only the night before the accident. And I hadn't cut it straight.

Rita began to describe each of the children's bedrooms and what they kept in them. She said that I had put something on Steven's bed that morning before going to see her, something to do with the USA and fighting. To be completely honest I could not believe what I was *hearing at this point, for only that morning I had put Steven's WWF (American wrestling) quilt cover on his bed. No one could have known that detail, as Steven's bedroom door was always closed and no one had been in the house that morning. No one could have known that I had changed the quilt, and how could Rita have known what was on it?*

Rita also told me that I was wearing jewellery that belonged to Vicky and then began to pick it out — four chains and six rings. And she was completely correct — she didn't get one chain wrong. She explained that Steven's grandfather came to visit once a week and left Steven a pound coin on the shelf if he was at school. I was dumbfounded, as he could have left the pound coin anywhere in the house, or even in his moneybox for that matter, but no, my Dad always insisted it had to go on the shelf.

After that first reading my life changed for ever. What she had told me had blown me away, so much so that I could have skipped all the way back home. I hadn't believed in mediums before and had been reluctant to go for the reading, and yet now, within the space of one meeting with Rita, my outlook had completely changed. My friends and family immediately noticed the difference in me. Before the reading I felt my life was worthless, I didn't know how to go on. But during the reading Vicky had told Rita that I should get on with my life because they were OK and happy. After hearing that I regained my strength and soon afterwards returned to work.

I went to see Rita again a few months later and she told me some personal things about Vicky — things that only Vicky and I knew. That day I had also put a pair of Vicky's socks on. They were under my boots and Rita couldn't have seen them, or indeed if she had, couldn't have known that they belonged to Vicky. But, of course,

Rita picked up on them and told me the exact words I used to say about them to Vicky, which was a standing joke between the two of us. As I was leaving, Rita stopped me and gave me a hug and told me to go out and celebrate, as it was Vicky's twenty-first birthday. It was a fact I had not told Rita during the reading.

I told my father about Rita and my readings. He was a sceptic and non-believer, but seeing the change in me he decided that he would also go and see her. During his reading Rita told him about the holidays he had enjoyed every year at Skegness with Vicky, Steven and me. She told him about Steven's baseball caps which he liked to wear. As she was telling him this she suddenly laughed and said, 'Why does he like to wear them the wrong way round?' Steven always wore his cap with the peak at the back. After that reading, Dad left Rita's and walked all the way home feeling on top of the world. The journey is actually only five miles but it was an enormous achievement for him as he suffers from bad health. He had always felt guilty about the fact that he was still alive while his two young grandchildren were dead, but the change in him following the reading was remarkable. He talked about it at the OAP club he attends and spoke to a lady who had lost her son in an accident. The lady visited Rita soon afterwards, and later thanked my father, saying it had changed her life around also. Sadly my father has since passed away, but I draw great comfort from the fact that he is with them now. I know that following his reading he was in many ways quite looking forward to dying so that he could be with them again.

Rita and I have become good friends since my first reading. She will ring me out of the blue and tell me that I am decorating again. Rita will tell me what paint colours Vicky has chosen and sure enough it will be the colour that I have already picked out. One time

I was thinking about putting a border up in one of the rooms in my house. I spoke to Rita and she said that Vicky was telling her that I couldn't make up my mind about which border to choose. She said, 'You can't decide between the paisley border or zebra-style print.' Rita was absolutely correct and I couldn't believe what I was hearing.

Rita also told me, on another occasion, that I was suffering from some pain in my legs and Vicky was worried about it. She advised me to see the doctor, which I did. He said it was being caused by my medication, changed it and now I have no problems at all.

About a year ago I appeared on a television programme called Q&A with Rita. *I hoped that my appearance on the programme might bring to other mothers and fathers who had lost children some sense of comfort and hope. I had, after all, suffered a double tragedy and yet thanks to Rita's reading had been able to turn my life around. But as it turned out the programme did nothing of the sort. Not only did they play the theme from the* Omen *films throughout the programme but they had a vicar on the show who said that I had been vulnerable at the time of the accident and shouldn't have gone to Rita, but should have turned to the Church. My answer to this, as I said to the producers of the programme afterwards – and I think that anyone who has been in my position will understand – was that it was God who took my children away and it was Rita who brought them back to me. I think any parent who has spoken to Rita would feel the same. Rita and I were furious about the programme, especially since it was so near to the anniversary of Vicky and Steven's death. All Rita had done was bring comfort, not just to me, but to thousands of other people. And all they had tried to do was to blacken her name and cause a great deal of distress to her and those people she has helped and continues to help. If anyone was taking advantage of anyone then it was the producers of this programme — not Rita. I know now that if it wasn't for Rita and her readings then I would have given up a long time ago.*

CURSES

When things repeatedly go wrong in our lives we talk of being jinxed or cursed. We wonder why we have suffered such a run of bad luck and may start to believe that there is a greater force at work which is, for some reason, punishing us. As a Romany I grew up believing in curses. I was taught that it was possible for someone to put a hex or a curse on you if you had done something wrong. To be honest most of the 'curses' I heard about were relatively petty – if someone had hurt your feelings or had taken advantage of you it was possible to 'make good' and cause something to go wrong in that person's life. These days I am not sure I do believe in the power of the curse. My grandmother always said that if something went wrong for me she would 'reverse it', but I think what she meant was that in a spiritual sense she would try and make things up to me. I don't think she would actually put a spell on someone who had wronged me.

I mention this here because quite often when people have had a very bad time in their lives they come to me and ask me whether I think they have been cursed. They can't believe life could deal them such a bad hand and therefore assume that they are being punished or made to suffer. Are they cursed? The simple answer to that is no, of course they aren't. The reason I can say this is because in my forty years of reading for people in situations like these there has never been any evidence in my communications with the spirit world to suggest otherwise. People who suffer from tragedy are unlucky and unfortunate but not cursed.

As I said in Chapter One, when we die we begin a journey towards spiritual perfection and when we enter the spirit world we are put on a plane that best reflects our behaviour in this life. That is when we are judged, when we are punished, when we are rewarded. It doesn't happen here on earth. So if your life has been afflicted by tragedy, please do not assume that you are cursed or that it is in some way your fault. It isn't. I'm afraid it's just life and life isn't fair.

We are always desperate to make sense of tragedy. Human nature forces us to seek explanations for everything in our lives. 'Why did this happen to *me*?' 'What have I done wrong?' 'Why is God punishing me?' 'I have suffered enough, why couldn't this have happened to someone else?' 'Where did I go wrong?' The fact is you can ask all the questions you want but there isn't an answer. Life is fated. We all follow a destiny, a path on which the major events of our lives are already mapped out for us. In an ideal world our parents will pass over before us and we, in turn, won't live to see our children die, nor they theirs. Our pain, our grief, our bad times will be staggered evenly over our lives so that we don't have to suffer too much at any one time. That way we would learn to cope with tragic events and have the strength to do so. But life, as we all know, is not like this. We can only hope that fate deals us a fair hand, and that if something terrible should happen to us then God will give us the strength to get through it.

Mary's story

Last year I received the following letter from Australia:

Dear Rita,

We have recently lost our beautiful daughter to epilepsy. To make it worse she was eighteen weeks pregnant, so it was double the loss with her baby girl dying too. She is our third child to die so you can imagine how distraught we are. Our first baby Danielle died of a cot death in 1982 and my son Bobby committed suicide in 1987 and now we have lost Emma. Please can you try and contact her and make sure that she now has her baby with her and is together with her brother and sister. Now I'm worried that my last remaining daughter Nicola and her son Brody will die, as it seems we are cursed for some reason. Please, please help me, Rita, as I am close to breaking point. I have to know my children are all together and are happy in heaven. I pray for you to help me, Rita,

Mary Jackson.

At the time I received the letter I hadn't planned to do any readings other than the ones that had already been booked, most of them months in advance, but when I read this letter I knew that I had to drop everything and make time for the woman who had written it. Here Mary tells her extraordinarily tragic story:

My daughter Emma died three years ago. She was nineteen and was four months pregnant. Her death left me absolutely distraught, not least because she was the third of my children to die.

I contacted Rita Rogers via New Idea *magazine. I wrote to her and asked her for a reading because I wanted to know that my children were OK. I needed to know whether I would see them all again and if they were in heaven. I had been to clairvoyants before, but at this stage I didn't need someone to look at my future, I couldn't care less about that – what I wanted was a medium to tell me that my kids were well and that I would one day see them again. This was the only thing that could bring me peace of mind.*

I lost my first child Danielle in 1982. She was ten months old, and she died of a cot death. I found her. My son Bobby took his own life in 1987 when he was nineteen. Two policemen arrived at my door one morning and broke the news to me. And then in 1999 our lives were turned upside down again when Emma died. Emma was an epileptic and had been on medication for years. Before her death she had come off her medication, against her doctors' advice, because of her pregnancy. We don't think she died from a fit – there is no evidence that she had one. When I found her in her bed one morning she looked as though she was in a deep peaceful sleep, but she was dead. It is thought that she suffered an adult cot death, a syndrome which is linked to epilepsy.

Naturally, I began to think that we must be cursed, and this was another question that I wanted Rita to answer.

I found the reading over the phone with Rita very helpful. There were so many things she seemed to know that she didn't get from my letter that I really felt I must have been communicating with my children. For example, Rita began the reading by saying that my mother was there and that she knew that I had lost 'her ring with the red stone'. When my mother died she left me her ruby wedding ring, and over the time of Emma's funeral I had lost it. I thought I had left it on the bedside table but it wasn't there and I couldn't find it anywhere. There were so many comings and goings in the house over that time that I assumed someone might have misplaced it or even gone off with it. But then Rita said that my mother was saying that she had Emma there with her, and that Emma was confessing to having borrowed it. Emma knew that I would never have lent it to her so she had borrowed it, worn it and was now saying that it was among her things. Rita said that Emma was laughing now and saying that she had taken my ring but that I was wearing hers. And I was! I was wearing Emma's ring on a chain around my neck. Rita couldn't have known all that. I was in Australia, she was in England and I hadn't put any of this in my letter to her.

Rita said that Emma was happy and at peace and that she had a baby girl with her. She said that her baby's name was Kylie Emma. Emma and I hadn't discussed what name she would give the baby when it was born, but 'Kylie' is the name of a very, very good friend of ours whom Emma was extremely close to. I just couldn't believe what I was hearing.

It was the details that Rita kept coming up with during the reading that shocked me and convinced me that she was talking to my children. Before my son Bobby took his life he made a point of telling his counsellor how much he loved me and that he wanted me to know this. Again none of this was in my letter but Rita came out with it. She said that he was telling her that I adored dogs as much as people, which is true, and that I was well known for this. When we lived at our old house it was something I was known for — I was *always coming home with stray dogs – and Rita was telling me that I often found them before they even got lost. Bobby also told Rita that I was more likely to talk to dogs than to my own husband, which is also true and something of a joke in our house.*

When I wrote to Rita for the reading all I wanted to know was how my children were, but now she was coming out with all this stuff and things about me. It was incredible. She was so accurate about little things and these are the things that convince you she is communicating with them. She said, for example, that Bobby kept telling her to call him Robert. Just before he went off to become a nurse he said to me, 'I don't want to be called Bobby any more, please call me Robert.' Rita also told me that Bobby was telling her that he had two Alsatians. He adored those dogs and walked them daily. She said that Bobby knew I had his watch and that I had given his bicycle away. This was true – I did have his watch and I gave his bike to my neighbours. She told me that he was very, very sorry about taking his life, that he had been very down but that he was at peace now and was with his sisters.

Rita said that I had been named after my mother. I was adopted and my mother's name was Winifred Margaret Mary. I don't like to be called Winifred so I have always been known as Mary. She also said that my husband did something with vehicles and that he drove a white van, often too fast. My husband works as a courier and he does indeed drive a white van.

Rita said that my baby Danielle had grown up now – she said this happens in spirit, young children grow to the age of twenty-one. She said that she and Emma were now friends and they were there together with Bobby and the baby. She said that Emma had lots and lots of shoes, which she did, and that I had photos of the children all over my house. She said that she knew we were moving house (again I hadn't put this in the letter) and she said this was a good thing as we had had so much bad luck in the old house. And she said that Emma was saying that she 'loved' the new house, which was significant to me, because Emma always went on about how much she hated the old house.

Rita also told me that the numbers 13 and 19 were unlucky for me. Well, 13 was the number of my old house where the bad luck had begun, something she can't have known because she wasn't given my address by the magazine. And Emma and Bobby were both 19 when they died.

Rita told me she knew this was my second marriage (again I hadn't mentioned this to her) and that my husband Robert was a lovely and popular man and a wonderful father. She said my mother was saying she had disliked my first husband, which was true, and that he had been a bad father.

At the end of the reading Rita told me that I would see my three children again but it wouldn't be for some time as I still had a long life ahead. But when I did pass away they would all be there to meet me. This was all I wanted to hear. The fact that Rita had been able to tell me so much more was an added bonus because it meant that my children really were safe and happy and in heaven.

Before my reading with Rita I had begun to think that maybe I was cursed in some way because I had suffered so much. I had lost three children and I had also had my fair share of problems before that, having suffered from polio and gone through a divorce. The deaths of my children had had a profound effect on me, each in a different way.

When my baby Danielle died in 1982 I was devastated. All I could do was sit and cry. For months I couldn't eat. I cleaned fanatically but couldn't do anything else. I was hit by this terrible, terrible grief and was just so, so sad, but I didn't feel any guilt. I had lost Danielle to a cot death – there was nothing that I could have done about it, nothing that I could have done to prevent it. And because Danielle was still just a baby I had given her nothing but love – there were no arguments or fights to regret, no instances that I wished hadn't happened. All that I felt was this awful, painful grief for my baby.

When Bobby died in 1987, five years later, I was just beginning to get back on my feet. Bobby was a wonderful, loving boy. I wasn't surprised that he went into nursing because he was very sensitive, and so loving, but he started to get very depressed. When he first went away into nursing accommodation he would call me for hour-long conversations – sometimes I couldn't get him off the phone – but later these conversations would become more difficult. He would call but would be very quiet, giving only monosyllabic answers to my questions. I'd have to force him to speak. When he came home one time he went out into the garden with the two German shepherds he loved so much. They had this habit of running ahead of you in the hope that you would throw them a ball, and Bobby, when he was well, would throw it to them, but that day when we were out in the garden and they ran ahead Bobby turned to me and said, 'See, not even the dogs want to be with me.' I couldn't believe he had said this – he knew they adored him, but I suppose in the depths of his depression he couldn't see this – so I turned to him and said, 'I hope you wouldn't do anything stupid, Bobby.'

Ask any parent who has a teenager what their worst fears are and the one thing they will say is being woken in the night with the police at their door. The police had been at our door before over the usual traffic and parking offences, but the moment I opened the door to them that day I knew in my heart that this wasn't the routine stuff. I thought it might have been my husband, maybe he had had a car accident. But it wasn't. It was Bobby. They had come to tell me he was dead.

When your child takes their own life you go through a very different kind of grieving process. There is so much anger, so much guilt and there are so many questions. Yes, there is the pain and the grief and the sadness, but it is very different, and so I grieved for my son in a way that I hadn't done for my baby daughter. There was this sense of loss, this emptiness and this awful guilt. I kept saying to myself, WHY? I wasn't surprised that Bobby had taken his own life but I was shocked. And then I went through the 'if only' stage. If only I had talked to him more. If only he hadn't gone to the nursing accommodation. If only he hadn't left home. You punish yourself with all these possibilities but it doesn't bring them back. All you are left with is emptiness.

In 1999 Emma died. It was midday and Robert, who had been working all morning, came to me and asked if Emma was up. I said I'd go and check. He said that was a good idea, 'She might be dead in her bed for all we know.' A light-hearted remark, that was all. Neither of us had any reason to know just how prophetic that simple statement would be. Emma was the second of my daughters to be found dead in her bed. I can't describe to you how awful it was, there just aren't the words.

Emma was an epileptic – she had suffered from fits before – and though she took medication we never thought for one instant that this illness would kill her, not unless she had a fit while driving a car or something like that. When Emma got pregnant her doctors advised her that she must keep on taking her medication. They said that more harm could come to the baby if she had a fit than if she took the medication, because if she did have a fit the baby might be deprived of oxygen. I remember arguing with Emma about this but she wouldn't listen. Emma was a very strong-minded girl and she was the type of person who wouldn't even take a paracetamol while she was pregnant. She would take all the folic acid she needed but nothing that she thought might harm her baby.

We don't believe that Emma died of an epileptic fit. When I found her in bed that morning she lay there peacefully, as though she were fast asleep. Had she had a fit the bedclothes would have come off the bed like they had in the past as she would have thrashed about, but she was still tucked in. The doctors believe she suffered an adult cot death – it's rare but it is connected to epilepsy. And now there are investigations under way to see whether cot death might be in some way genetic. Perhaps this might explain both Emma's and Danielle's deaths.

Robert took Emma's death very badly. Out of all the children we had lost, this one hit him the worst. I think that he had rationalized the deaths of Danielle and Bobby, but Emma's death was so sudden, so out of the blue. It shocked us all. Emma and Robert were very close, they adored each other, and with his pain came guilt. You see, his study, where he was working that morning, was right next door to Emma's room. He couldn't believe that he had been working there all morning while she lay dead next door. He went through the 'if only's' this time. If only he had gone in and checked on her earlier. If only he had woken her up when he started working, and so on.

After Emma's death I went through some kind of breakdown. Three years later I am still on Prozac. On a good day I can just about manage the housework. We have a video of Emma at her debutantes' ball and a cassette recording of the funeral service (in Australia they tape services) but we haven't played them yet. I think it would just be too upsetting for us.

To say the deaths of my children have changed my life is an understatement. I used to be very social, I loved to go out and meet people. Now I very rarely leave the house to see people. I used to laugh a lot. Now the only thing that makes me laugh is watching the sitcom One Foot in the Grave. I suffer from deep depression and have no hunger for life at all.

Rita told me during the reading that I had a good marriage. She said that I had been lucky because in her experience nine out of ten marriages collapse when children are lost. She said that we had survived this because we shared our grief and this was a good thing. Robert and I are lucky that we have survived all these tragedies, but perhaps one of the reasons for this is that we realize that we each need our own space to grieve and that people grieve in different ways and at different times. As I said, I have become more withdrawn since this all happened and don't really like going out. Robert on the other hand is a very popular person and he finds it helpful to be around others. He deals with his pain on a daily basis by keeping himself busy. He will visit the children's grave every two weeks (both Danielle and Bobby were cremated but we decided to bury Emma, and when that happened Robert moved the ashes of the other two and put them with Emma, so now they are all there together, Danielle, Bobby, Emma and our grandchild) and take flowers. If he has a problem he will go to the grave and talk to Emma. I prefer to put flowers around their photographs. I don't like going to the grave, as Rita said the children aren't there, but we all do things in different ways.

In my letter to Rita I said I was worried that something might happen to our daughter Nicola given the luck we had had. She assured me she would come to no harm as the others were looking after her now. Rita mentioned Nicola had been through a bad time and that she had been quite 'naughty' in the past. This is true. Nicola did go through a bad stage when she fell off the rails and got into a bad set. I guess that was just her response to what had happened. Nicola's grief meant getting angry. The pain eventually has to come out in some way. Rita said that she had got better and this is true, but it's tough to be in her position – she has watched our family life fall apart and disintegrate. We always used to have wonderful family Christmases, for example. Emma loved Christmas and so there would be a huge tree and piles and piles of presents, but after she died I couldn't cope with it. That's been hard for Nicola and also her nine-year-old son, Brodie, who has all these memories of how it used to be. But we have learned to adjust. This year she is taking him off to Queensland where they will go to all the amusement parks and enjoy the sun. It's very hard being the child left behind. You end up having to compete with the memory of your sibling. You may think that your parents don't care for you, or loved the child who has died more than you, so imagine how tough it was for her.

Although my life is not what it was, I believe that Rita's reading and her books really have saved me. I have been a Catholic all my life, albeit a lapsed one, but to be honest I have gained no strength from my faith. I pray and I believe in God, but I am still haunted by the fact that it was God who took them from me. The deaths of my children destroyed my life, but Rita's reading was a turning point and made me feel better. When I asked Rita whether I had been cursed she said no. She said that I had had three very special children who were too good for this world. Each of them touched people's lives in their own special way.

Now I know that my children will be waiting for me when I die and will be there to collect me. I know I have to be here and I have a life here with Robert, Nicola and my grandson. I wouldn't want to take my own life, but knowing that we will all be reunited one day means I am no longer scared of dying.

Having the knowledge and the proof that my children are in spirit and happy has given me a sense of peace. I decided to contribute to this book because if my story can help at least one person then that's wonderful.

11. *How to Cope with Someone Who Is Grieving*

Throughout this book I have talked about learning to live with the death of a loved one and the pain that accompanies such a loss, but in this chapter I want to move away from that subject and talk about learning to live and cope with someone who is bereaved.

In Western culture death is a taboo – most of us find it a difficult topic to talk about. Any allusions to death in our everyday conversation are seen as macabre, mawkish or morbid. Death is not a subject people want to bring up, discuss or dwell on. Furthermore, death itself is shrouded in so much ritualistic secrecy that we very rarely confront it as part of our lives. As a result, when death does come into our lives we aren't very well equipped to know what to do or say about it.

In other cultures and religions there are very defined rules and points of etiquette on how to behave around someone who is grieving. It is made obvious in some way that the family is in mourning, perhaps by what they are wearing or how they conduct themselves at home, for instance. There might be structured times when it is appropriate to visit the grieving family, and times when it is not, or a time when it is appropriate to pay your respects to the one who has passed away by visiting the body or making an offering. There might even be a code of practice as to what someone should say to the bereaved in these circumstances.

In our culture we don't really have these structures any more. People may wear black for a funeral as a mark of respect, but they won't sit round in it for days on end, let alone months like they used to. In the Victorian age people took to wearing either black or a simple black armband, not just as a mark of respect for the person who had died, but so that *other* people would know that they were in mourning. By wearing black a person would be telling society that they were grieving and therefore they would avoid embarrassing social situations.

These days there are no social codes to help us. There are no rules as to how we behave once someone has passed over. When a loved one dies, some people ask for flowers to be sent to funerals, for example, whilst others prefer charitable donations; some folk want private, family-only funerals, others like memorials. This is all well and good, but the problem with this is that people really don't know how to behave around death. People feel uncomfortable around it, and so they feel uncomfortable around those who are mourning that death. Time and time again I get letters from people asking me what to say and how to behave around someone who is grieving. I always say that it depends on the individual, what has happened and what the relationship between the one who has passed over and the one who is left behind was like, but there are some basic pointers I can give on how to cope with someone who is grieving.

The first piece of advice is that anyone who is at a loss as to how to cope with someone who is grieving is *don't, whatever you do, avoid them because you don't know what to say to them or how to act around them.* Don't isolate them in their grief but offer them comfort, time and support. Even if you don't know what to say you can help someone in the initial stages of their grief by doing something practical for them. Making food for them, or helping with shopping or domestic chores is a way of showing that you are there for them in their time of need.

People who are mourning are living with the reality of their loss twenty-four hours a day, seven days a week. It is the only thing that they think about. If you avoid them you are just adding to their pain. People who are grieving *need* love and support. Crossing the road to avoid having to talk to someone who has just lost a loved one is going to hurt them more and make them feel more isolated than they do already. If you really can't think of anything to say just go over and give them a hug or say that you are very sorry. Following the terrible and tragic deaths of Holly Wells and Jessica Chapman in Soham in the summer of 2002 their parents issued a joint plea for people not to avoid them or 'shun' them if they saw them in the street. They asked people they knew to act normally around them. They said just a nod or acknowledgement would do. If they wanted to talk they would, if they needed to be silent it would be obvious, they said. This plea was no doubt helpful because not many people know how to react in a situation like this. What can you say to these poor people that could possibly help? How can you show just how much you are with them? The answer is by being there for them, by saying hello, by sensing if they want to talk or just need an acknowledgement.

My second piece of advice, an important point, is *don't pretend that nothing has happened*. Most people are so unsure about what to say to someone who has lost a loved one that they assume that it's better to say nothing at all. This is probably the worst thing you can do. People who have never lost anyone close to them might think it's best always to change the subject when the name of the person who has died is mentioned in conversation, but what they don't understand is that most people don't just find it important to talk about that person, they actually enjoy it. Remember that the bereaved person has just lost someone they have loved very much and remembering them and talking about them can help fill the awful hole. Talking about those we have loved and lost keeps them alive for us.

In the first few weeks of their grief the bereaved person might not be ready for long heart-to-hearts about what they are going through. They might become quite withdrawn and silent but a few words of love and comfort from you can really give them strength and let them know that they are in your thoughts.

Try to avoid clichés such as 'Time will heal' or 'You'll get over it'. When you have just lost someone you love very much, you know that you'll never get over it and that time won't heal you. These platitudes are really quite dismissive and belittle the emotion that the person is going through. It is much better to say that you have no idea what they are going through but you are there for them, or to say something about the person they have lost, or that you knew how much they loved that person.

People often shy away from writing letters of condolence because they don't know what to say. These letters can be difficult to write but they mean so much to the person who has lost their loved one. They offer comfort and support and for the bereaved person they keep the memory of the person they loved alive. The best letters, I find, are those filled with stories and anecdotes about the person who has gone. It is nice for a parent who has lost a child to receive letters from school friends which are filled with memories, for example, because it creates an even bigger picture of the child they have lost. If you didn't know the person who died well, don't think you shouldn't write. A simple letter of support to the bereaved person can mean so much. And if you don't know what to say, or perhaps are too upset yourself to write a long letter, send a card letting them know that they are in your thoughts and prayers.

As I said in Chapter Two, people grieve in different ways and the pattern of grief is never formulaic. Try and understand what they are going through, be sensitive and be very patient. If someone is feeling angry or resentful about their loss, be prepared for the fact that they might lash out at you. Try not to take it personally – understand that they don't mean it, they just need an outlet for their emotions. You need to respect what they are feeling and give them time and space.

In my experience the worst time for a bereaved person usually occurs after the funeral. Before the funeral the bereaved person is caught up in the shock of their loss and with funeral arrangements. During this time there are always people around, things to do, plans to make, but afterwards, when we all return to our routines, they are left with this awful emptiness and that's when the reality really starts to sink in. This is the time when you really should be there for them. If you can't be physically with them, then keep in regular contact by telephone or letter.

Keep the memory of the person who has passed away alive for the bereaved. As time passes the bereaved person will want to talk more about the person they have lost and will feel more comfortable doing so. The reason for this is that they are usually scared their loved one will be forgotten and their memories of that person are getting further and further away. It can be a very cathartic experience.

THE GRIEVING CHILD

It is very difficult telling a child that someone in the family has passed away, especially if that person has had a very close relationship with the child. I dreaded telling my girls that their father had passed away and wondered how on earth I was going to put it to them. When I did tell them he had gone, I said that he had gone to heaven. I didn't want them to think that they were never going to see him again, or that they had been abandoned, so I made a point of telling them that though they couldn't see him, he could see them and loved them all very, very much. The older girls understood what I was talking about and had realized that their father had been ill and in hospital, but at five Kerry was much too young to have taken any of this in. I sheltered her from the news until after he was buried. I remember that at the house later when everyone had gathered for tea and drinks following the funeral, Kerry asked me whether we were having a party. Of course, children have their own logical way of seeing things and can be quite pragmatic. I remember Mandy looking me straight in the eye when I told her that Dennis had gone to heaven and saying to me, 'But Mummy, what about his fishing tackle? He hasn't taken it with him.' I had to assure her that he would get a whole new set there. And Kerry said on the first Christmas following Dennis's death, 'If I send all my toys back to Santa will he send my daddy back to me?'

Most people like to say to a child that the person who has died has simply 'gone to heaven' or become an 'angel' because they were so special. People who do not hold these kinds of beliefs say that the person is now 'at peace' or has even 'gone away for a while'. Any of these euphemisms will do, but try and avoid words such as 'dead' or 'killed'. Children don't really understand the concept of death and are always frightened about things they have no experience of. There is also too much finality associated with the word. Remember that you want to give the child the belief that they are still living on.

It is very important to make sure that it is a loved one who breaks the news to them. There is nothing worse than hearing it from a stranger, from a friend in the playground or even, for that matter, from a teacher. If they are at school at the time, try to go there yourself, or get a loved one to collect them, and then break the news. That way you will be able to decide what you say and how much detail you give them.

Children crave normality and routine, so when someone close to them dies, particularly if it's a parent, they get very upset and worried about what will happen to them in the future. Even if everything around you is falling apart, try to ensure that everything seems normal to the child. Try to stick to their regular mealtimes and bedtimes if you can, make sure you are there to collect them from school and that people they love are around them as much as possible. I think it is sensible to allow them some time off school as they adjust to what has happened, but not to leave their return to school too long. They need their routine and their friends around them. And on a purely practical level, you need some time to yourself too.

It's very important to keep the memory of the person alive for children, especially if they have lost a parent or a sibling. If they are very young they may not have many memories themselves so it's up to you to keep their loved one alive for them. There is nothing that children like more than a story, so telling them about what their daddy, mummy or sibling was like when they were alive will help the child and can also be quite a cathartic experience for you. In the same way, make sure you tell them how much their loved one adored them and would have been proud of them. It's a nice idea to make a memory book about the person who has passed away, by filling a scrapbook or album with photographs, letters and stories about the person who has died. Alternatively you could create a memory box and fill it with all these things and little objects and knick-knacks too. Either way you will have created something for the child to keep and remember their loved one by.

Some people believe that funerals can be too harrowing and traumatic for young children. The sight of a coffin and lots of people dressed in black can be very upsetting for a child and I really don't think it's a good idea for a young child to see a coffin being lowered into the ground. It can be frightening and I am not sure that a young child needs to see that. However, children do need to be able to say goodbye. If they are excluded from the ritual of the funeral they may have trouble accepting that their loved one really has gone from their lives. If they are not going to attend the funeral service, try and arrange something that they can get involved with. If you are religious you might want to take them to a church and ask your priest to say a special mass or service for the loved one. If you are not, you might think of taking them to the sea or some special place where they can take flowers and say goodbye. Or you might think of creating a memorial for them, something that they can get involved in. I like the idea of planting a rose bush or a tree because they can help with the planting and watch it grow.

THE GRIEVING TEENAGER

Young children are quite resilient and may adjust to their loss more easily than an older child partly because they have less understanding of what death really means. Teenagers on the other hand can be deeply affected by the loss of a loved one. Not only are they old enough to understand what death means but they are also fully aware of the knock-on effects such a loss might have on their lives. In the case of a teenager who loses a parent, not only will they mourn them but they will worry about their future. They might worry that you are going to move house, or away from your neighbourhood, for example. They might be concerned about your financial situation, or the prospect of you remarrying. Teenagers do seem to worry a lot about things like these. The reason for this is because they are at a very sensitive age. Keep reminding yourself that whilst they might look and act very grown-up, deep down they are just little babies. I find that a death in the family can really bring out the child in a teenager, so don't leave them alone to get on with it, or assume at any stage that they are coping just fine. Make sure you give them lots of love and affection and the forum to be able to talk about anything that is saddening or worrying them.

I get a lot of letters from parents who are concerned about the way their teenage child has reacted to a death. Some say that their child is angry, others say they won't speak or are moody and unresponsive, acting as though they just couldn't care. In more extreme cases parents tell me how their child has gone 'off the rails'. Although it may not seem so at the time, all this behaviour is completely normal. Teenagers are very volatile and full of raging hormones. At the best of times their behaviour can be erratic and unpredictable, so imagine what it is going to be like at a time like this!

All the behaviour patterns I have mentioned above are expressions of grief. The surly teenager who just doesn't seem to care really does care deep inside. They might be shrugging off their pain in front of you, but inside they are hurting. Be patient in this situation, don't force any emotion out of them, wait for it to come in its own time, because it will. And in the meantime make sure that they know you are there for them when they want to open up. The angry teenager is venting his or her pain and hurt by trying to blame someone else for them – this is emotional transference. This teenager's pain needs to be channelled in the right way so try talking to them about what has happened but be aware that they might easily direct that pain at you. If they do, try not to take it personally. As for the child who has gone off the rails try not to be judgemental. The last thing you should do is get heavy and punish them, but on the other hand you must let them know that their behaviour is unacceptable. It's a delicate balance. I think the best way of dealing with this situation is to be as patient as you can and to keep talking to them. Let them know that you are hurting too and that what they are doing is just making you feel worse and not allowing you the time to mourn properly. It may take a while to get this message through but it is worth persevering.

Teenagers really do need their role models. It is very hard for a teenage girl to lose her mother because she needs a woman to talk to as she goes through these difficult years. Likewise it's hard for a boy to lose his father. I think it is very important to appoint someone you know and who your children like to act unofficially as a surrogate role model. I am not suggesting that they try and be a parent figure, but I think it is important for your child to know that there is someone around they can turn to other than you when they need help or advice or simply a chat.

Another thing I come across quite often is the way teenagers like to fill their dead parent's shoes. When the father passes away the older boy will be quick to assume the role of man of the house, while the girl who has lost her mother might suddenly start fulfilling a greater domestic role. This is always very endearing so long as it doesn't go too far. Remember that your teenagers need their childhood. They might have your best intentions at heart, but they need to get on with their lives.

The most important thing to take into consideration when coping with a bereaved teenager is that this may be their first experience of death and loss, so make sure that you are patient, and be there for them whenever they need you.

THOSE MOURNING A CHILD

As I have said in Chapters Three and Four, the death of a child is one of the worst things that can happen to anyone, partly because it breaks the natural order of things. The grief we go through when we lose our young is incredibly intense and heart-wrenching.

People who lose their children will go through an extreme range of emotions while they grieve and you should be prepared for this. They might be numb and in shock, angry or resentful, tearful or depressed. Some people become suicidal, and however irrational it may seem, most parents feel guilty at some stage in the grieving process.

All you can do as someone who cares for this person is be there for them every step of the way and allow for the fact that their mood will swing. There will be times when they don't want to talk and they need their space, times when they need to sleep for long stretches, periods when they suffer from insomnia or suffer from severe anxiety attacks. They might show their grief quite physically, not just by crying, but by rocking or sitting doubled over as though they have been hit in the stomach. They might want you to hug them, but remember there are going to be times when they cannot bear to be physically touched. They might be feeling so angry that they take it all out on you. They might be so numb that they behave as though nothing has happened at all.

When someone is going through this kind of grief you have to be prepared for anything and realize that you are in for the long haul. This pain isn't just going to disappear after a few months – it's going to be with them until the day they die. In my experience, people are always wonderful when someone dies – up until the funeral. Then people go back to their own lives, which is of course completely understandable. Life does move on and so do we. But for the grieving parent life doesn't move on like ours. They are trapped in a horrible recurring nightmare which they cannot wake up from. Try and remember this and realize that they are going to need you, in some capacity, long after the funeral flowers have wilted.

Be sensitive too to how deep their wound really is. They might at some stage feel up to socializing or going out. They might return to work or to their old routine. But remember that whilst they may be acting normally, nine times out of ten it's a brave face you're looking at. Behind that smile at the office, at the shops, in the street, at the pub or party is a very wounded person trying their best to enjoy life once more. Always bear that in mind. If they suddenly want to leave a social situation, let them. If they can't cope with strangers at parties asking whether they have children, then understand this. Don't *not* invite them to your party, because this would be even worse. Just allow them the choice – and the chance to refuse, even if it's at the last moment.

People who lose children, in my experience, are totally obsessed with the memory of their child and have a terrible fear of losing that memory. They feel that once they have lost it they will have lost their child for ever, so a very good thing you can do for someone who is in this situation is help keep that memory alive.

You can do this simply by talking about the child when the person is ready. As I keep saying over and over again, you can't airbrush a person out of your life just because they are dead. When the grieving parent is stronger talk about their child a lot. Tell funny stories about them, ask questions about them and so on.

Another way you can help keep a child alive for a grieving parent is by encouraging them to keep their child's anniversary. Whether this be their birthday or the day they passed over doesn't really matter. Giving someone flowers is a nice idea because it not only shows that you remembered, which will mean a great deal to them, but they can also take them to the grave or put them up at home near a photograph of their child.

Be mindful that landmark holidays and red-letter days can be hard for parents who have lost children. Very often there is a deep reluctance to celebrate anything, be it Christmas, Easter or other people's birthdays. Try to remind the parent that the spirit of the child would want them to celebrate these kinds of events because children love parties and holidays. Be mindful of the rest of the family too. If the parent has other children, they must try, hard as it is, to keep going for them. The parent might not want a big tree with lights and presents at Christmas, but the other children will. Depriving them of what little happiness there is left in their lives is, in my mind, selfish. We have to be strong and we have to move on for others.

If a child has died while they were at school or at college, I think it's a very good idea to create some kind of memorial for them there. This could be anything from a rose bush, a garden, a school or college prize to something more elaborate like a water fountain. It doesn't really matter what it is, but I do find in my readings that spirit children like this sort of thing. They very rarely visit their graves – why should they when there is nothing there – but they do like to visit their friends and the places where they had a life. A memorial like this is a very good way of keeping a child alive for those left behind, and this would give other children a focus for their grief.

Lastly, the most important advice I can give to anyone who knows a bereaved parent is to be careful what you say. Never ever say to someone who has lost a child, 'I know how you feel' or 'I can imagine your pain'. Unless you have lost a child yourself, you simply cannot begin to fathom how painful this kind of loss is. It is truly indescribable and making this kind of comment will not help the person who is suffering. Very often the people best equipped to help the grieving parent are people who have been through the same thing themselves. There is a wonderful charity called the Compassionate Friends, which I am a great supporter of. The Compassionate Friends puts grieving parents in touch with each other so that they can talk about their experiences and share their grief. There are branches of this organization all over the UK and Ireland. If you live abroad, I am sure that there are similar organizations operating where you live, so do a little research, because it could prove very helpful.

THE GRIEVING SOULMATE

In my experience people who lose their soulmates often feel very lost and lonely. They feel as though they have lost part of themselves and often become a shadow of their former selves.

They could be nineteen, they could be ninety – the pain and feelings are just the same.

If the person has been living with their soulmate, they may find it incredibly difficult to adjust at the most mundane domestic level. They might not be very good at looking after themselves, they may not be good round the house, be able to cook or to cope with the shopping or the bills and things like that. One way you can help someone who has lost a soulmate is by helping them with these sorts of things. Of course people need their space, and you have to respect this – they might be proud, or feel they don't want to be a burden to anyone – but we can all do with a helping hand from time to time, so stepping in to ease these kinds of domestic duties can be a good thing to do, and can help ease some of the stress which seems to accompany this kind of grief. Even babysitting for the kids or getting them out of the house so that the grieving person can have some time on their own can be the most tremendous help. It's little things like this that show the person that you care.

Another thing to remember is that the person who has lost their soulmate has lost their companion. No longer do they have someone to go on holiday with, to eat dinner with, to arrive at a party with. If you have both been asked to a social occasion, you could suggest that they come with you as this will remove some of the fear of being on their own. If you are taking a holiday, suggest that they join you, or if you are cooking a meal for yourself, why not ask them over. You can't bring their soulmate back, but what you can do is help lessen to some degree the drudgery of a life alone.

Grieving soulmates always tell me that what they miss most

is having a special person to talk to. When we are in a couple we tend to take it for granted. Whether it is first thing in the morning or last thing at night, there is always someone there we can confide in – it could be something we are worried about, it might be something nice. If you know someone who has lost their soulmate and you have the time, it's a nice idea to call them quite often for these kinds of chats. Remember that they don't have anyone special to talk to any more. If their child is having a problem at school, for instance, they no longer have a partner to discuss it with, so if you can allow yourself to become their sounding board that could be very helpful.

THOSE WHO HAVE LOST A FRIEND OR SIBLING

Adults who lose friends and siblings can become very depressed. If their friend or sibling has been close to them in age it can make them acutely aware of their own mortality, which can upset them further, but the main thing to remember is that they have lost someone they were once very close to and this can create a great hole in their lives. Of course you cannot and should not try to replace the person they have lost from their lives, but you can help fill that void by letting them know that you are always there for them.

Another problem that happens when people lose a friend or a sibling is that they tend to get sidelined in what I call the 'grieving pecking order'. When someone dies we tend to think of those closest to them. We worry how their parents are feeling, their children or their soulmates and we direct our sympathies towards them. We send our letters of condolence to these people, we ring them to see how they are, we visit them and talk to them about their grief – and we forget about what their brothers and sisters, friends and colleagues are going through.

Just because these people are not as immediately related or linked to the person who has passed away doesn't mean that they aren't suffering just as much as the parent, the child or the soulmate. They might be feeling the pain of this loss just as intensely. The girlfriend of the teenager killed in a car crash, the best friend of the cancer victim who was there through the illness at every moment, the sister of the father of three who has died, the man who lost his colleague and friend in the plane crash: all these people are really suffering the loss of someone who had played a pivotal role in their lives.

It is really important not to forget about these people when someone dies – they are all hurting and grieving. Next time you sit down to write a letter of condolence, remember these people too. Call up the man who lost his drinking pal when you are going to the pub on a Friday night, and invite him out with you. Talk to the girl who lost her boyfriend and see if she is OK. Ask your friend who has lost their colleague if they need to talk about it. When someone dies it isn't just the immediate family that are affected, so always keep that in mind.

THOSE MOURNING A SUICIDE

For some reason suicide is such a taboo subject that we never know what to think or say about it. I get so many letters from people who have lost loved ones to suicide and tell me how upsetting it is that people don't give them enough support when they lose someone in this way. I don't for one moment think that this is because people don't care – of course they do. They just don't know what to say about it. People get very embarrassed about suicide. They are not sure how they should react, and so they just don't mention it at all. They avoid any reference to the person who had died and by doing so brush the whole thing under the carpet. This can be extremely hurtful to the person who has lost their loved one.

Whether someone takes their own life or not is irrelevant. Someone you know has lost their loved one, they are upset about it and that is all there is to it. As I said in Chapter Nine, the majority of suicides are actually accidents. Most people don't really plan to take their lives – they are making a desperate cry for help and sometimes it goes wrong. The ones that really did intend to take their lives did so because they were at the end of their tether, they just could not cope with life any more and they needed to be at peace. Basically, these people are extremely ill. They may not be suffering physically, but they are suffering so badly mentally that they are driven to suicide to put an end to their pain. If you think about it, you wouldn't ignore the death of someone who had died of cancer, so why ignore the death of someone who is clinically depressed.

In my experience, people who lose loved ones to suicide need just as much if not more support than anyone else because the people who are left behind always suffer from so much guilt when someone takes their life. They need to be told that there was nothing they could have done, they need to be made to realize that they couldn't have prevented it and they need to understand it wasn't their fault, and the life of someone who has committed suicide should still be celebrated no matter how tragically it ended.

THOSE MOURNING AN UNBORN CHILD OR STILLBIRTH

Just because a child has died before being born into this world, or has been stillborn, does not mean that the child never existed. Our children are with us from the moment they are conceived, for that is when the soul is born. People who lose a child through miscarriage or have a stillborn child are just as prone to grief as if that baby had lived to see the world. The mother who loses a child in either of these ways will have been very aware of the baby living inside her while she was pregnant, and the father who has been looking forward to the birth will also feel this loss.

People often make the mistake of assuming that parents in this situation aren't grief-stricken. Of course they think that the loss is sad, but they may not fully comprehend the extent of the sadness that it has caused. When mothers lose babies through miscarriage, the grief they suffer can often be delayed – they might not realize how sad they are until many months after they have lost the baby. People should be very aware of this and realize that at some stage the mother might want to talk about her loss. Bearing a stillborn child can also be very traumatic. Remember that the mother has carried that baby for nine months. She may not have been aware of any complication during her pregnancy and the loss of the baby at birth might have come as an awful shock. In other cases she may have known that the child was not to make it and will have had to carry the dead child and go through the terrible ordeal of giving birth to it.

Situations like these can put a terrible strain on a couple. In some cases the mother may be so wounded that she forgets that the father is hurting as well, but she should remember that she does not hold a monopoly on grief. The mother may also go through feelings of guilt and think that she is in some way to blame for the loss of the baby. Similarly the father of the child, unable to show his emotion, may try to pretend that nothing has happened. As I have said, men and women grieve in different ways.

The best way of helping a couple in this situation is to be aware of what they are going through and to be there for them when they need you. Don't make the mistake of brushing the incident under the carpet or saying, 'Don't worry, you'll have more children.' Hopefully the couple will be able to conceive again, but always remember that the new child doesn't replace the one who has passed over. No two children are the same. The child who has been lost cannot be replaced, and any new child that is born is not a substitute.

THOSE CARING FOR THE DYING

Nursing someone who is dying is very difficult. When we know that someone we love is terminally ill it is natural for us to want to do all that we can for them. We don't want their last days here to be uncomfortable, we don't want them to be afraid or in pain, and so we care for them, we nurse them, we keep them company, we talk to them, we hold their hands and we tell them everything will be all right when we know that it won't.

When you are caring for someone who is dying, take it one day at a time. It can be a very draining experience, both emotionally and physically. I find that people who are in this position put on such a brave face for the person who is dying that they often end up going into denial. They get to the stage where they refuse to accept that the person won't make it or that no miracle cure can be found. Likewise, the dying person puts on their own brave face to spare their carer's feelings. They know full well that they haven't got much time left here, but they don't want to worry anyone by looking scared or like they have given up hope. This can be very tiring for both parties. The problem for the carer is that it masks the pain that they are going through inside. If you are caring for someone who is dying, then you need to be cared for by someone yourself. You need a release, someone to talk to, some place to go for air when you are not at the bedside.

The other thing I have noticed is that people who have cared for a dying person take the loss very badly indeed. Whilst they might say to you that it's OK because the person is no longer in pain, deep down they are really at sea. If you think about it, someone who has cared for a dying person has spent a great deal of time with them – they may have been keeping a vigil by that person's bed twenty-four hours a day – so when that person dies they have a very large gap in their life. The time that they would have devoted to caring for the dying person will now be empty and it is very likely that they will become quite depressed and feel redundant or even that they failed in some way. If you know someone who is in this position, try to be there for them as much as you can. Taking them for a walk or for something to eat while they are nursing will provide a welcome break for them, and once they have lost their loved one, try to be there as much as you can to look after them. This is, after all, the time when *they* will need to be cared for, loved, nurtured and looked after.

12. *Learning to Live Again*

Just because someone has died doesn't mean that they have gone for good. Your loved one may have passed away, but they aren't that far from you. They have simply slipped away for a short time. They are in another room waiting for you, waiting for the time when you will be together again. When that moment comes you will be together for eternity.

Your loved one hasn't died, they have just passed over. They aren't in that grave you keep, they are all around you. And even though you cannot see or hear them, know that they come to you with love and warmth.

If you come to see death like this, then I think you will find it easier to accept and live with. A belief in the afterlife won't stop you from grieving and hurting – believe me, I have shed many a tear for those I have lost – but what it does give us is a sense of hope and peace. We no longer fear for the ones we have lost. We know that they are happy where they are. We know that they are not alone. We know that they are not lying cold in their graves but are around us. We know that this isn't 'it', that there is a life after this.

I hope that what I have written in this book and the stories people have told have shown that the spirits of our loved ones are always with us. You don't have to visit a medium to know this – just look around you, look out for the signs, feel their presence.

People who lose someone close to them often say 'My life won't be the same again,' and to some extent they are absolutely right. If we lose someone we love very much, then of course our lives are not going to be the same. We have to accept that their death is going to have a profound effect on us, but though our lives aren't going to be 'the same', that does not mean they have to be worse. Of course there will be a period when we feel that our life is over, when we feel so much hurt and pain, but in time those feelings will get easier to bear. We don't recover from the loss of a loved one, but we can learn to live with the pain.

In order for us to live again, we have to learn to see things differently. We have to understand that there is hope and there is a future. We have to learn not to mourn the death but to celebrate the life we knew. We need to learn how to rejoice in the people we knew who were taken from us, and look forward to the day when we will see them again. We have to stop thinking about it as our 'loss', and see it for how it once was – our 'gain'.

If we learn to see the world like this, if we learn to see life and death this way then we can learn to live again. And that is what our loved ones in the spirit world would really want for us.

0203 312 1070